WICKED FAIRYTALE'S COLORING ADVENTURE

Where the Magic Never Ends.

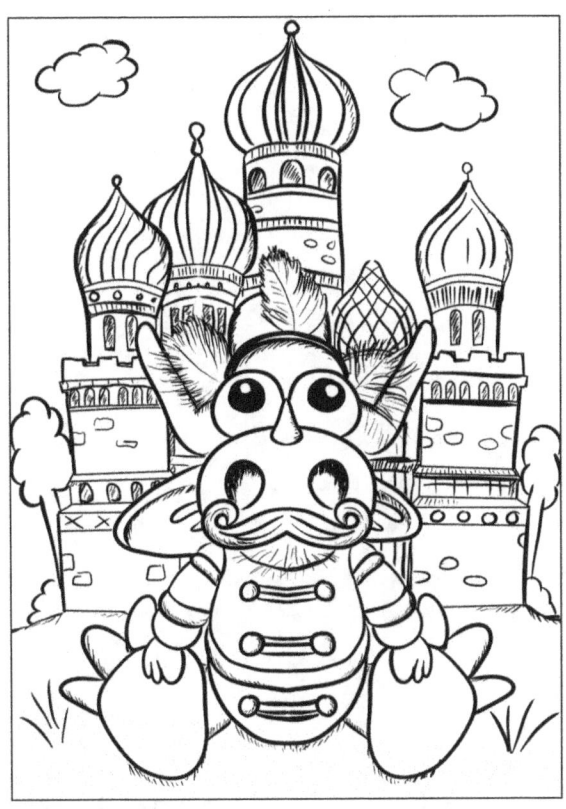

Designed & Created By: Tara Marks

Authored By: Tara Marks

Illustrated By: Ulf-Johan Virtanen

Dedicated to everyone out there that has an inner child and dreams of Dragons.

A special thanks to everyone who believed in me, especially my Moose.

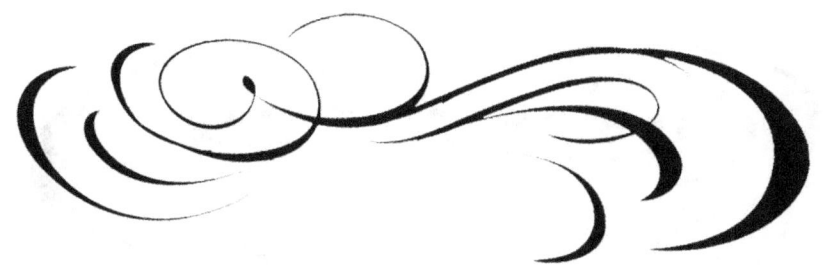

OH HOW SHE LOVED BOOKS, ALMOST AS MUCH AS SHE LOVED DRAGONS. BUT BOOKS ABOUT DRAGONS AND DRAGONS THAT HAD BOOKS WERE TWO OF HER MOST FAVORITE THINGS OF ALL.

- The Shadow Trilogy

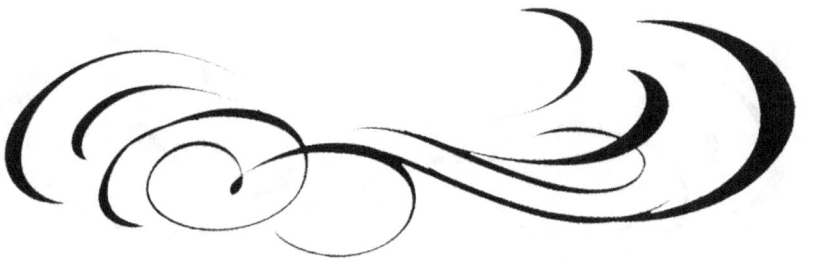

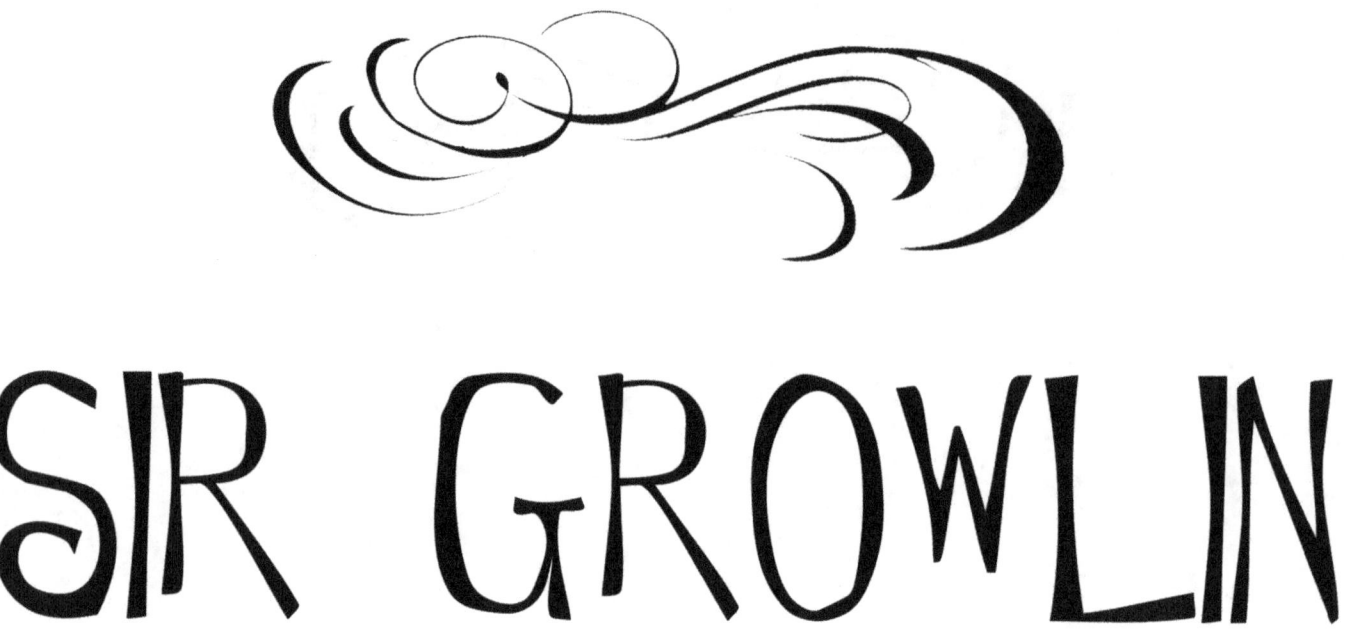

SIR GROWLIN

Growlin is a Magical Creature and his type is known as a Trollie (pronounced trolley). Trollies are mischievous little things who find refuge in closets, bathrooms, basements and other dark places when they are in need of a hiding place while in trouble in the magical realm. He is an odd collector of human socks and can be very temperamental also, having a perpetual scowl on his face no matter his mood. Marked by the Fairy Queen, ultimately Trollies can cause no harm to a human but Growlin has been known to cause havoc on plumping and electrical systems in houses where he is not welcome. He's very vain, egocentric, and pouty and coupled with his loud stomping, has been known to be the thing that goes "bump in the night". Typically around two feet tall, he is only seen by those who possess the Fairy Gift of Sight.

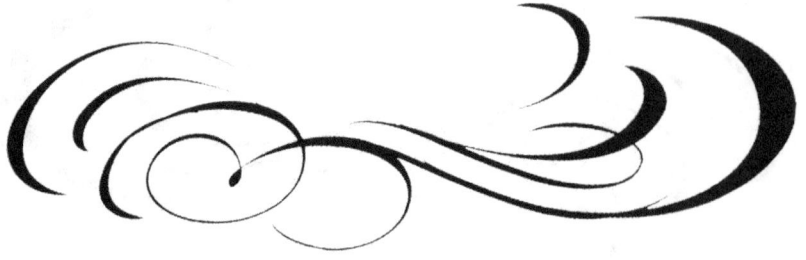

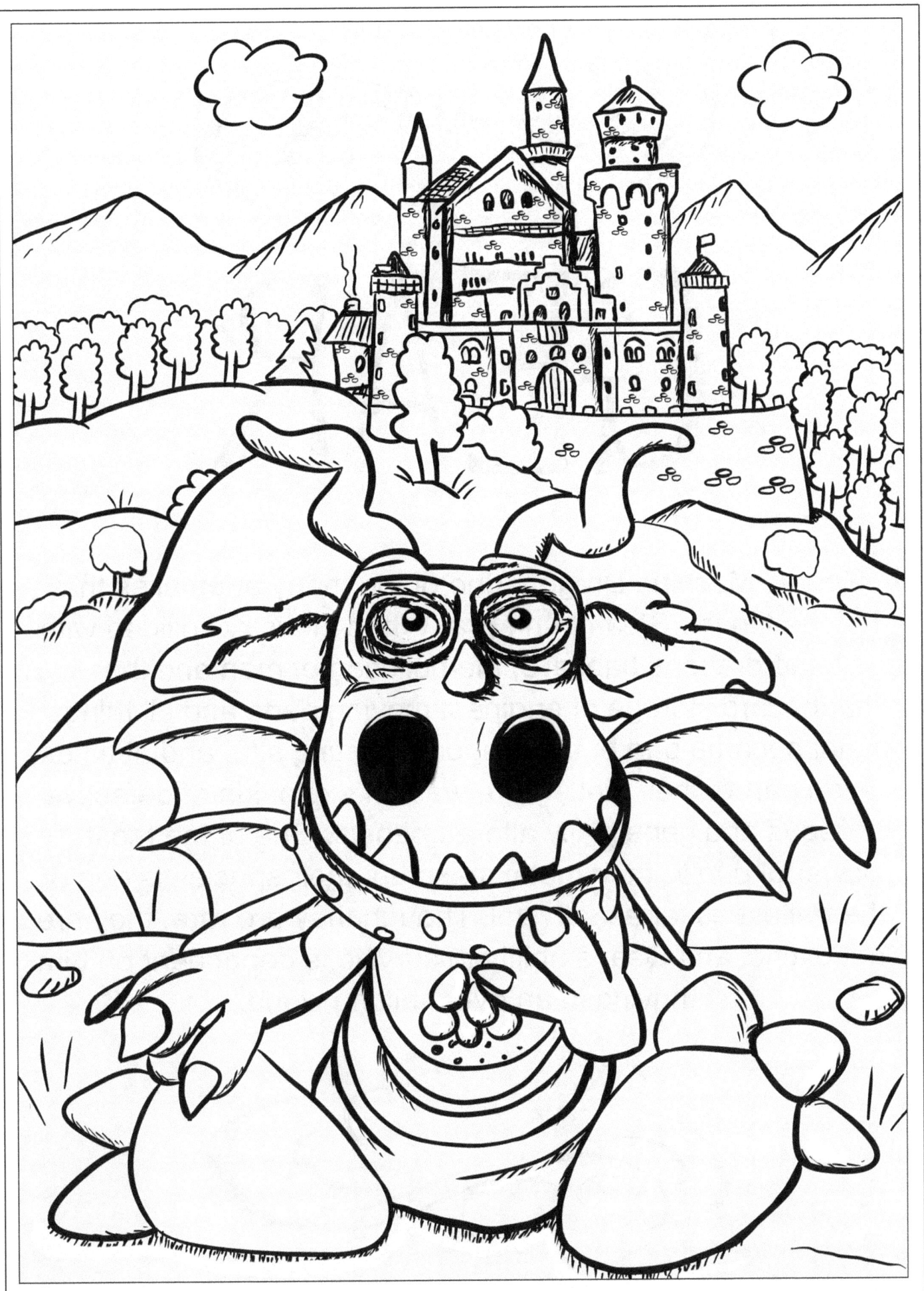

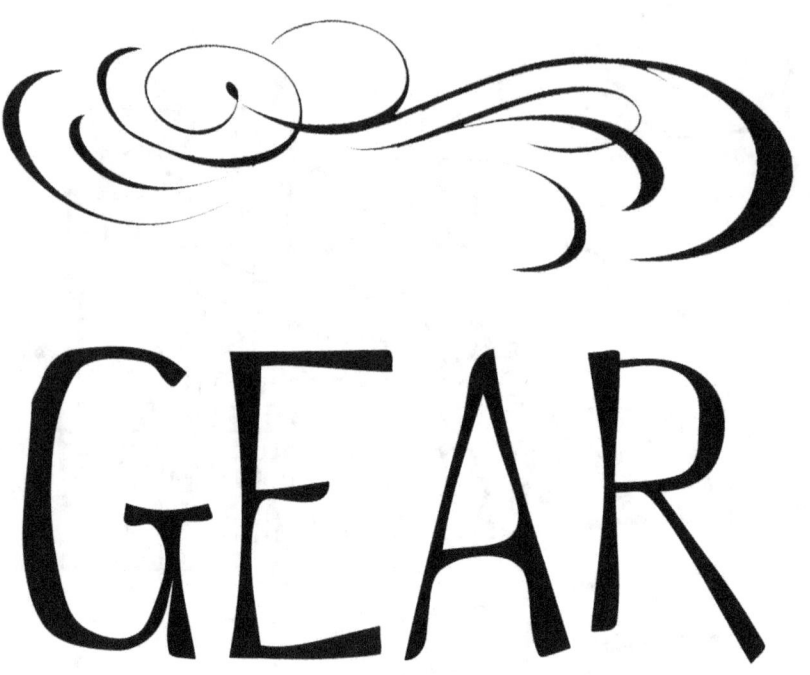

GEAR

Gear is Machine Dragon, one of the many anomalies that hatched in the Steampunk Era. When industry collided with the dragons habitat's, the pollution of man and the haphazard storage of engines, moving parts and all things metal became part of the dragon's nesting site, and at times, even part of their diet. There was an explosion of defective eggs and genetically altered beasts. One of the most powerful due to their metal make up, their species is one of the frailest as far as survival. Though they are rare, they are not extinct and Gear's ability to survive is dependent on him thriving in an ever shifting world.

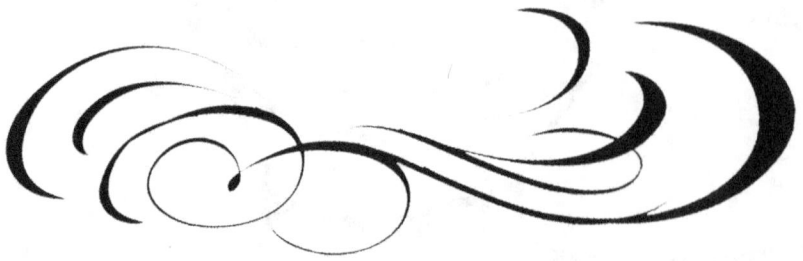

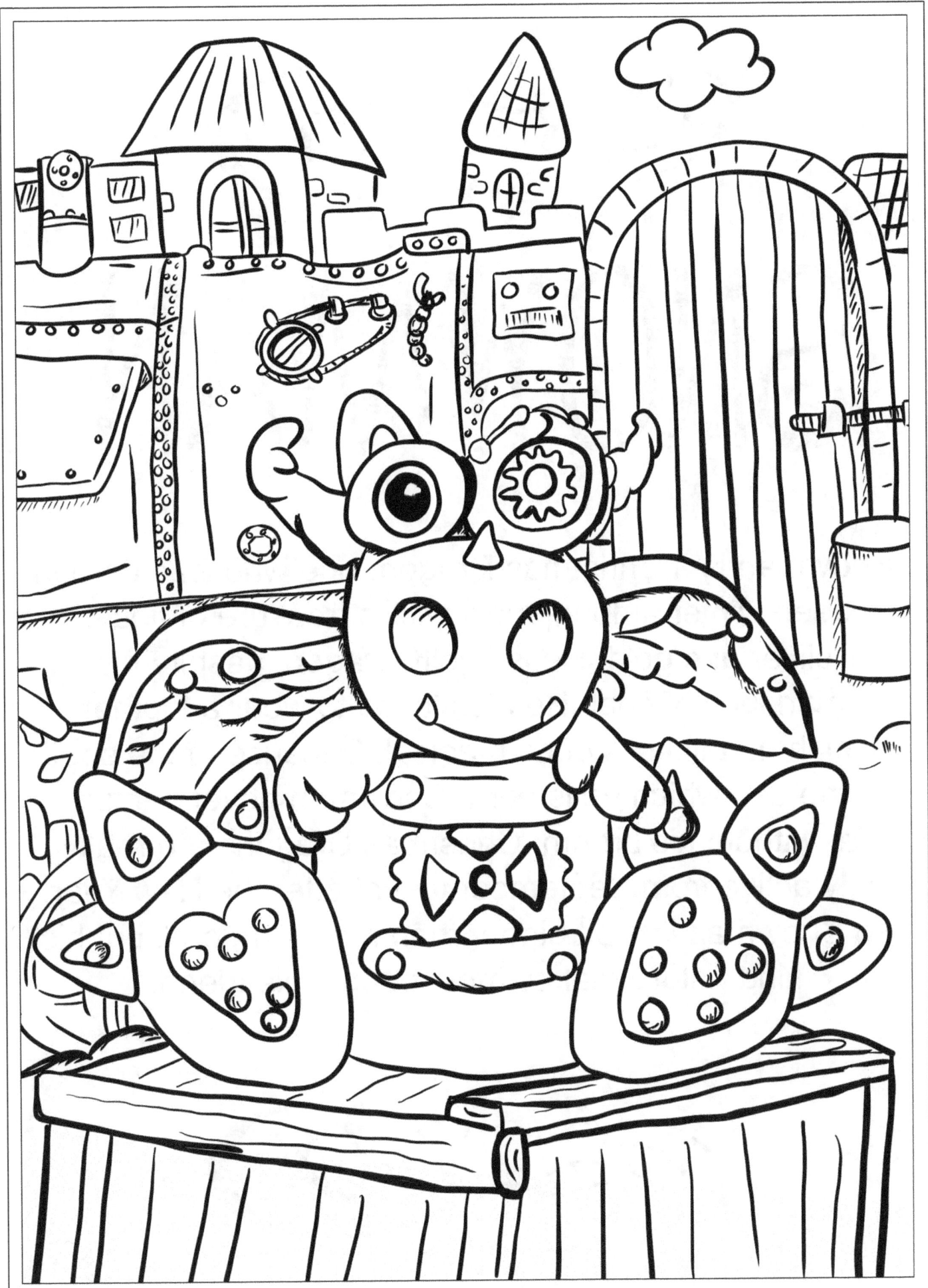

SNOWMAN

Snowman is a Christmas Dragon, one who was born in deep winter among snow with a treasure of tinsel, silver and gold. He is a jolly dragon, despite his markings of coal. He also loves to wear a top hat which he thinks is quite magical. Because of the soot in the den which he is born, Snowman never ventures far without his broom. Christmas Dragons are really only active from September to just after the New Year, so Snowman is a bit bigger than most dragons, but his kind nature makes most people his friend.

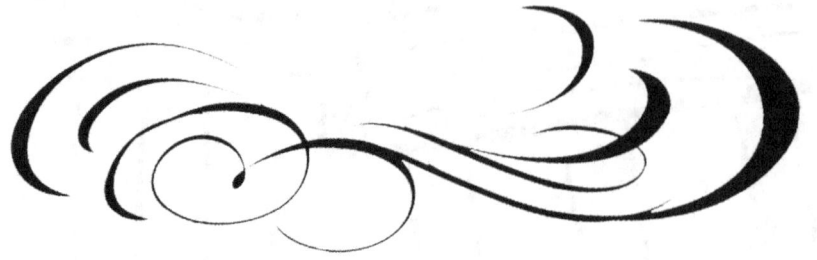

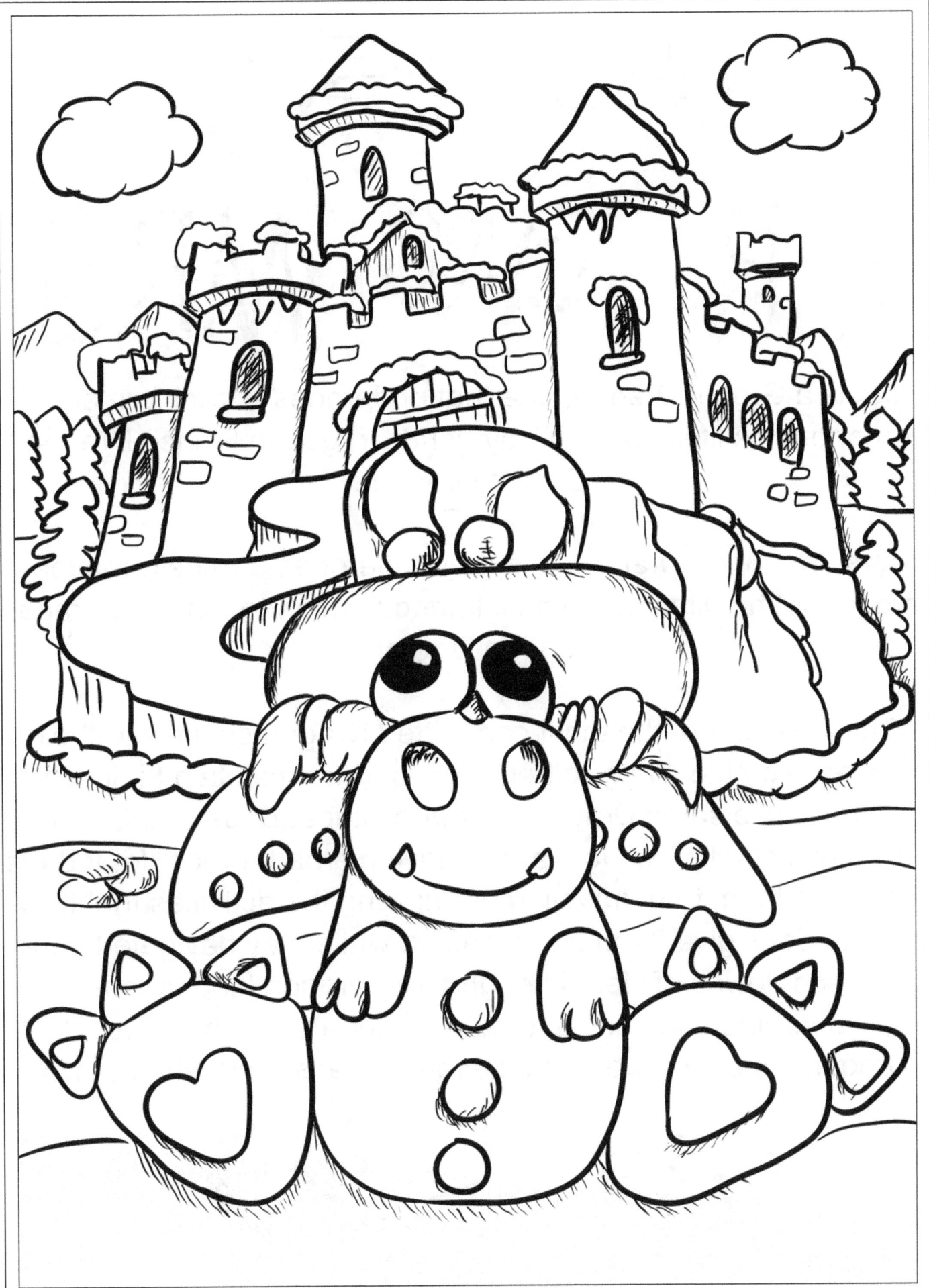

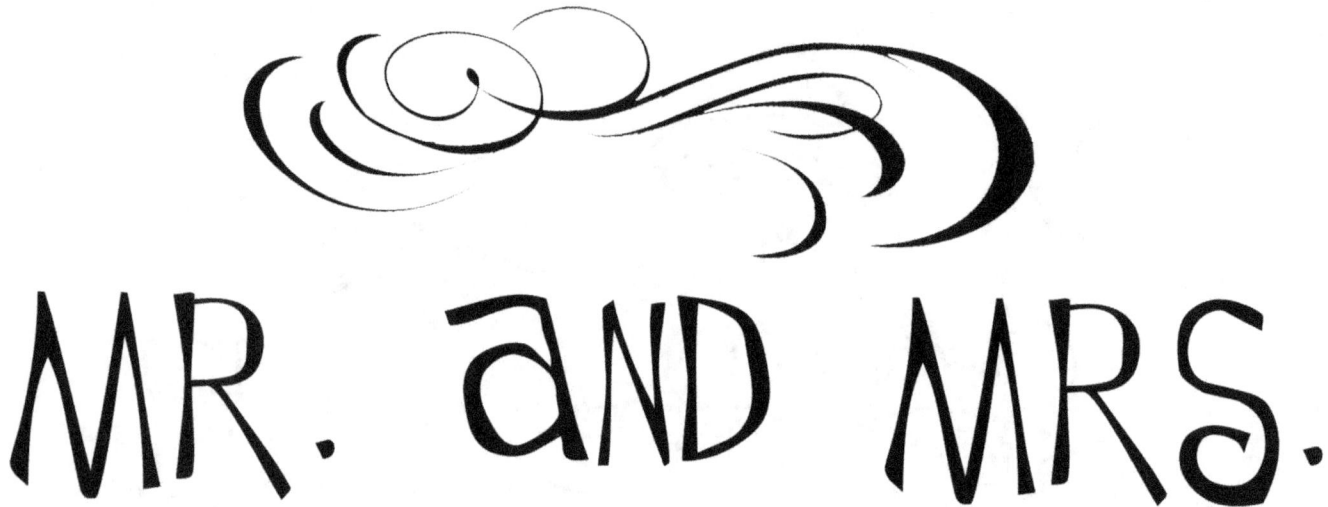

MR. AND MRS.

Mr. is a Groom Dragon, one that undergoes a transformation throughout his lifetime from Boyfriend Dragon to Fiancé Dragon to Groom Dragon.

Mrs. is a Bride Dragon, one that undergoes a transformation throughout her lifetime from Girlfriend Dragon to Fiancée Dragon to Wife Dragon.

They are one of the most committed Dragon species to their mates, with the ability to help their partner maintain their cozy cave. While some Dragons prefer solitude, Bride and Groom Dragons actually look forward to having a partner for life. It does not keep them from traveling or enjoying the activities that they love but does give them a companion while they navigate the ups and downs of life. Although most Dragon language is undecipherable and seems to be only understood by mates, these Dragons utter two words that even humans understand, I Do.

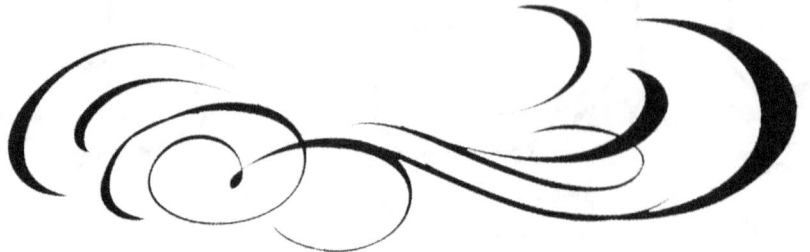

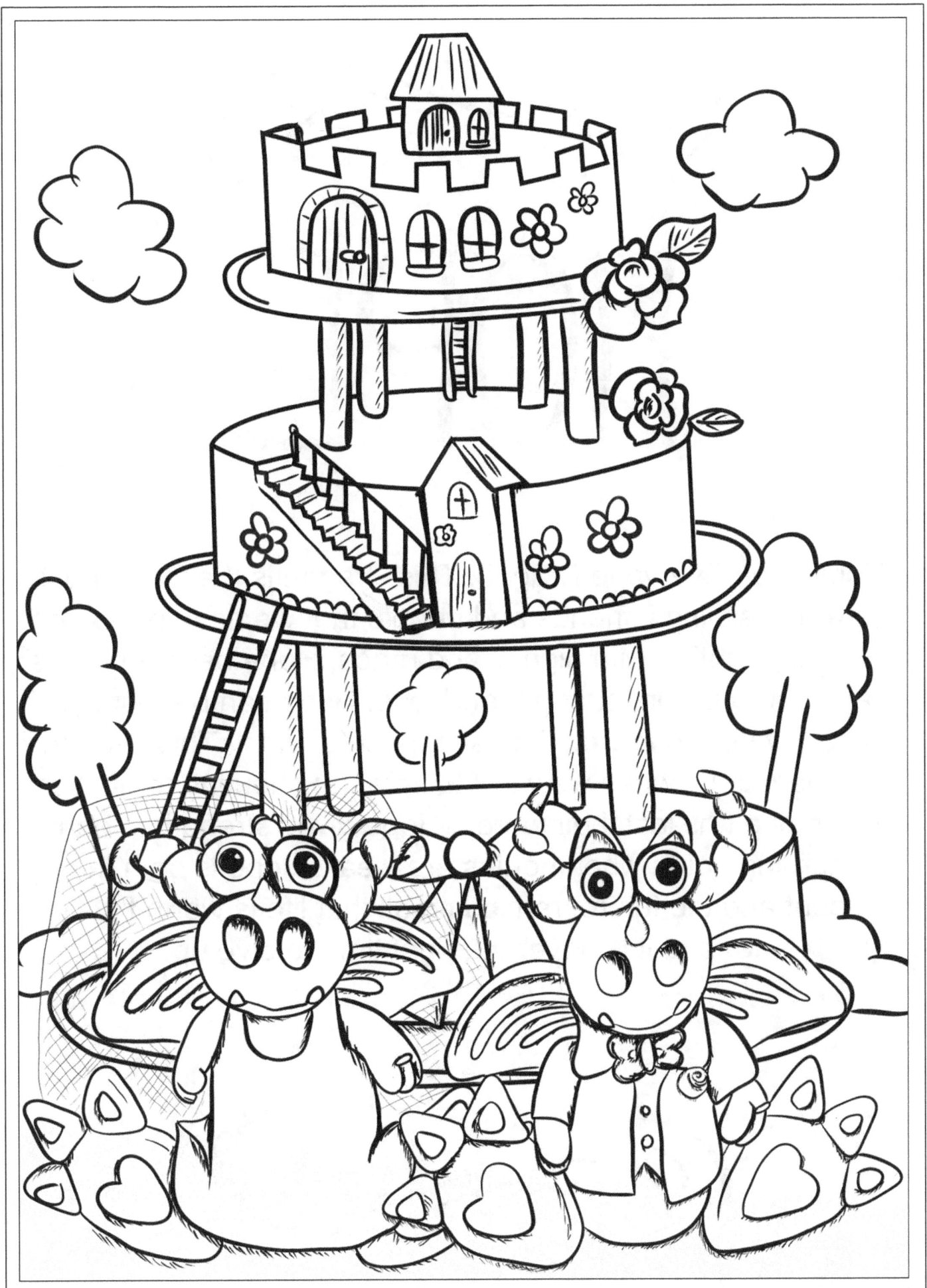

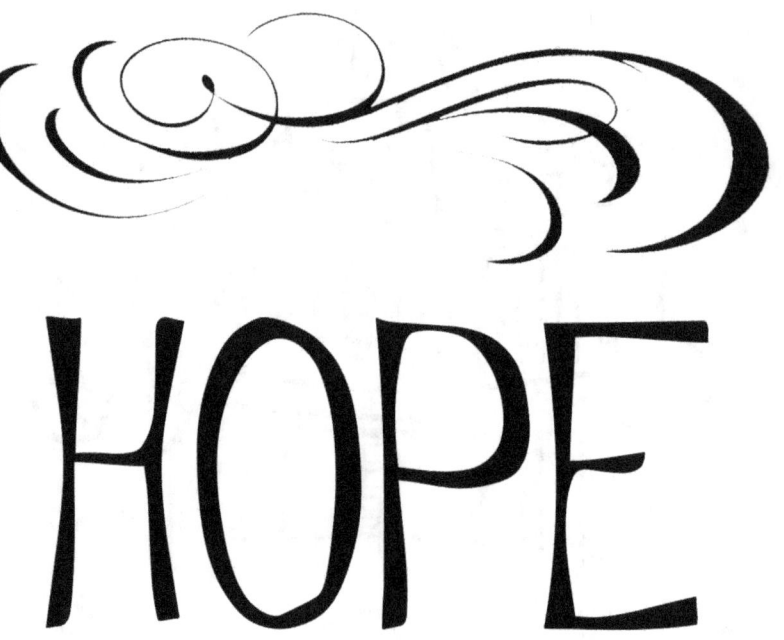

HOPE

Hope is an Everyone Dragon. This Dragon is the face of our parents, siblings, friends and people that we have not even met yet. Fighting with dignity and grace, Hope begs for cures and compassion, strength and love. Hope can be found in places where one would least expect to find it. This Dragon whispers to us when we want to scream; shouting for justice when one has lost their words. Hope gives strength in early morning hours when bodies are weak. Hope is both the present and the future, reminding all that life is worth fighting for and it is never the right time to give up.

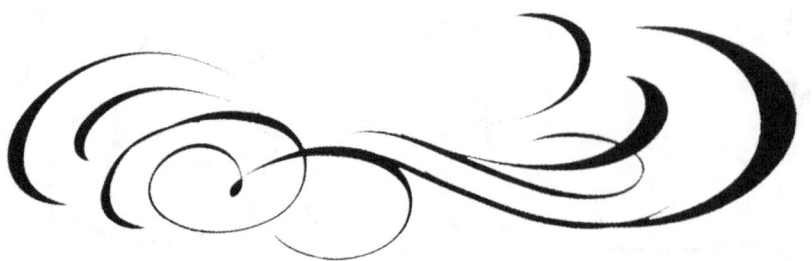

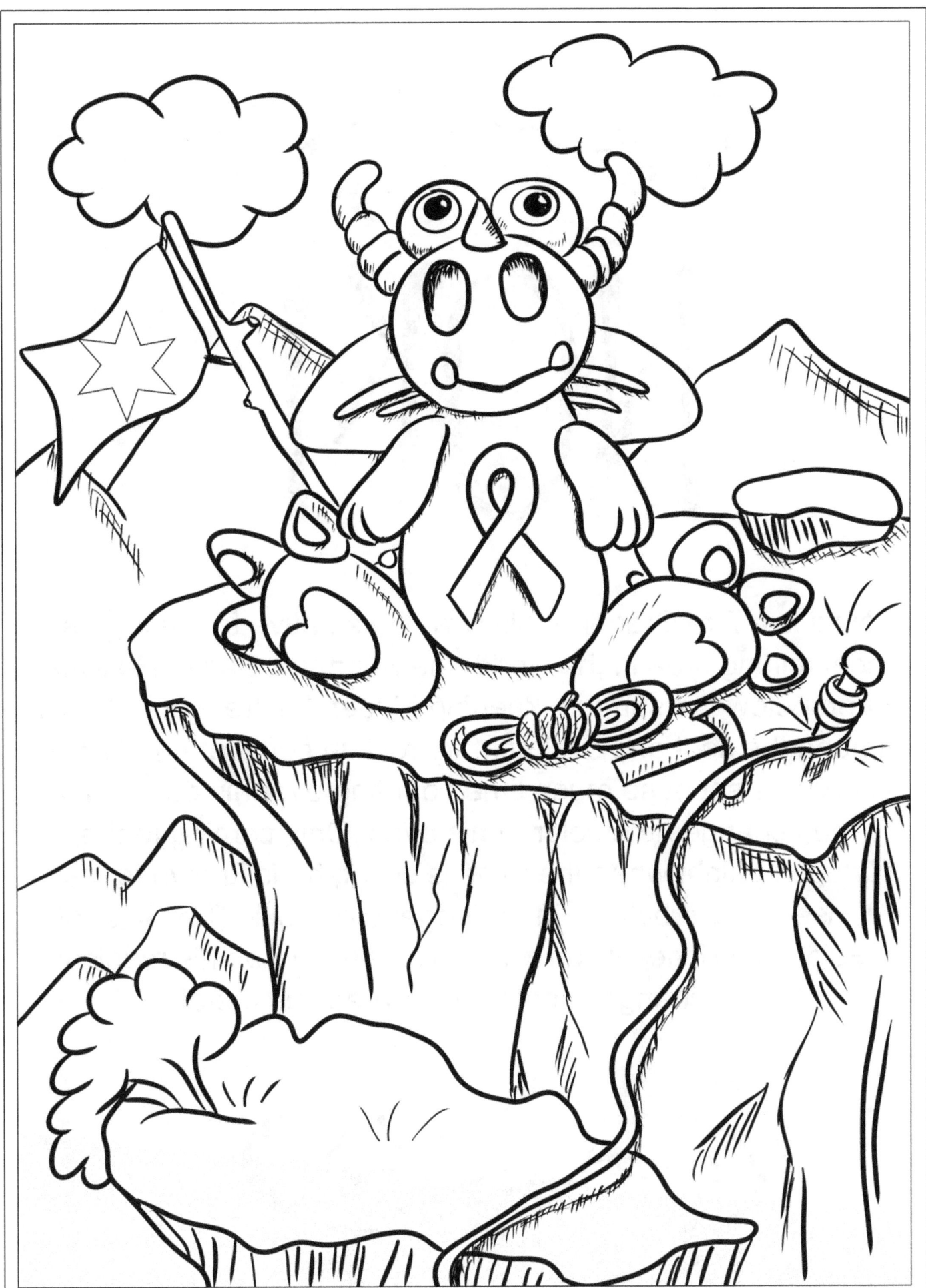

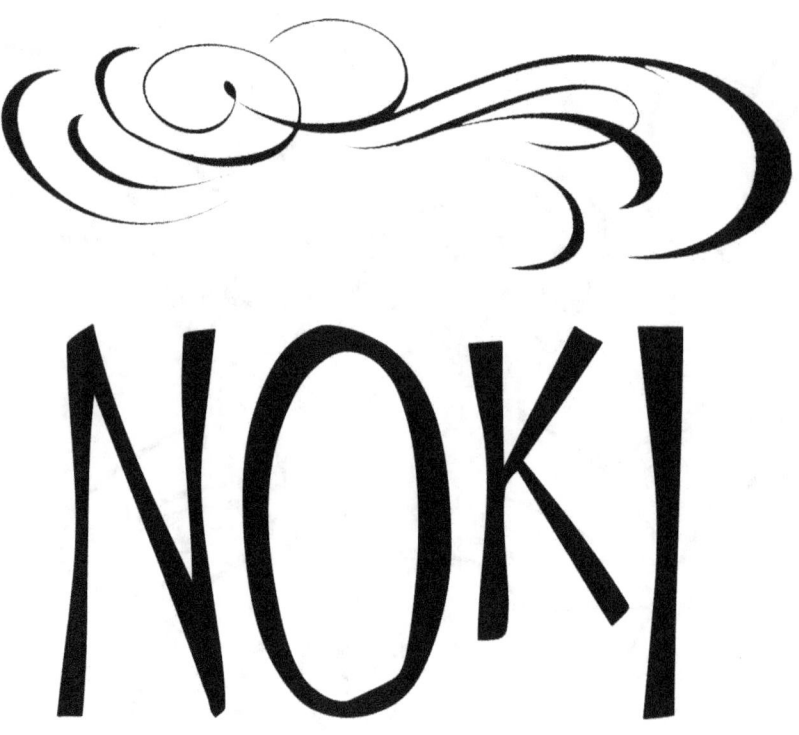

NOKI

Noki is a Fire Dragon. This Dragon is native to the largest coal mining area in the world, the Kuznetsk Basin. He lives deep below the surface, keeping hidden his treasure of gold among the soot and sedimentary rock in complete darkness. Noki has spent so much time counting over his gold that it has changed the color of his eyes. Only coming to the surface at night when the mine is silent, he is known to bless those in need believe in the Legend of Noki- The Giver of Gold. He will never run out of his treasure, as his magical fire changes coal into the precious metal.

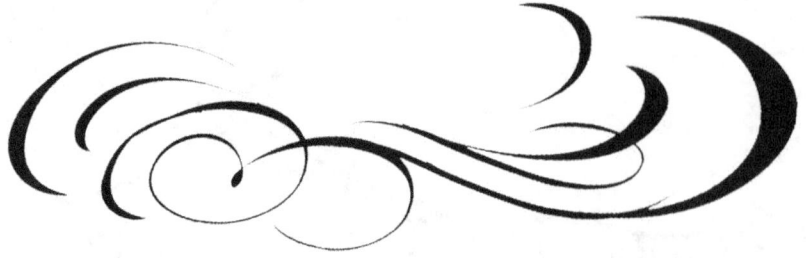

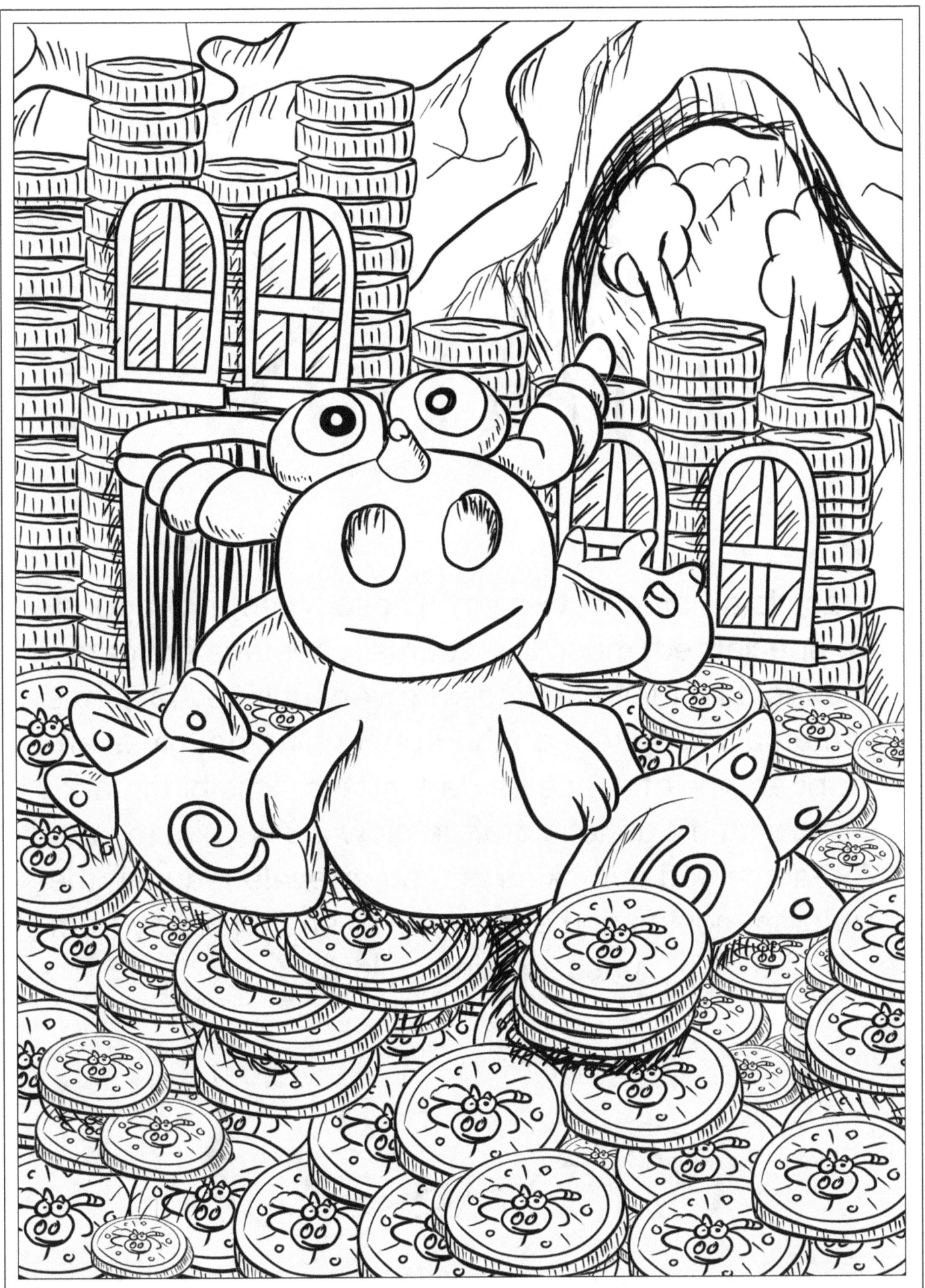

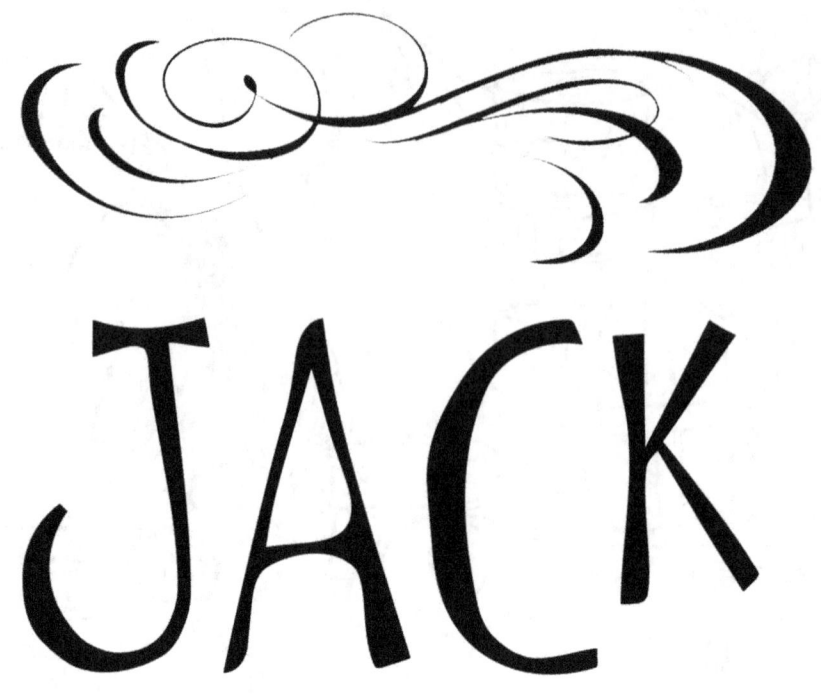

JACK

Jack is a Pumpkin Dragon. These types of Dragons are specialized, much like zebras, cheetahs or tigers in the fact that their markings are very unique. Jack has an amazing pattern on the front of him that gives an appearance of a face on dark nights. This birthmark, along with his genetic orange glow allows him to pass for the carved pumpkins that are prevalent during the autumn months and allows him to snatch candy from unsuspecting children.

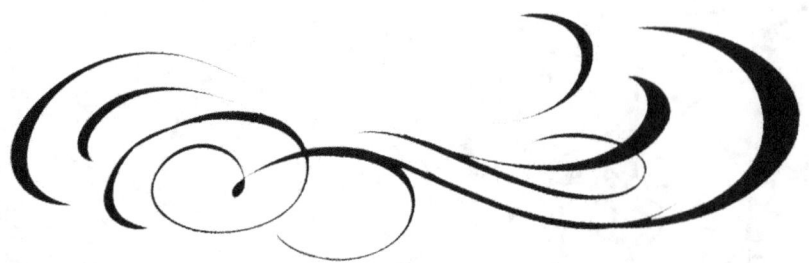

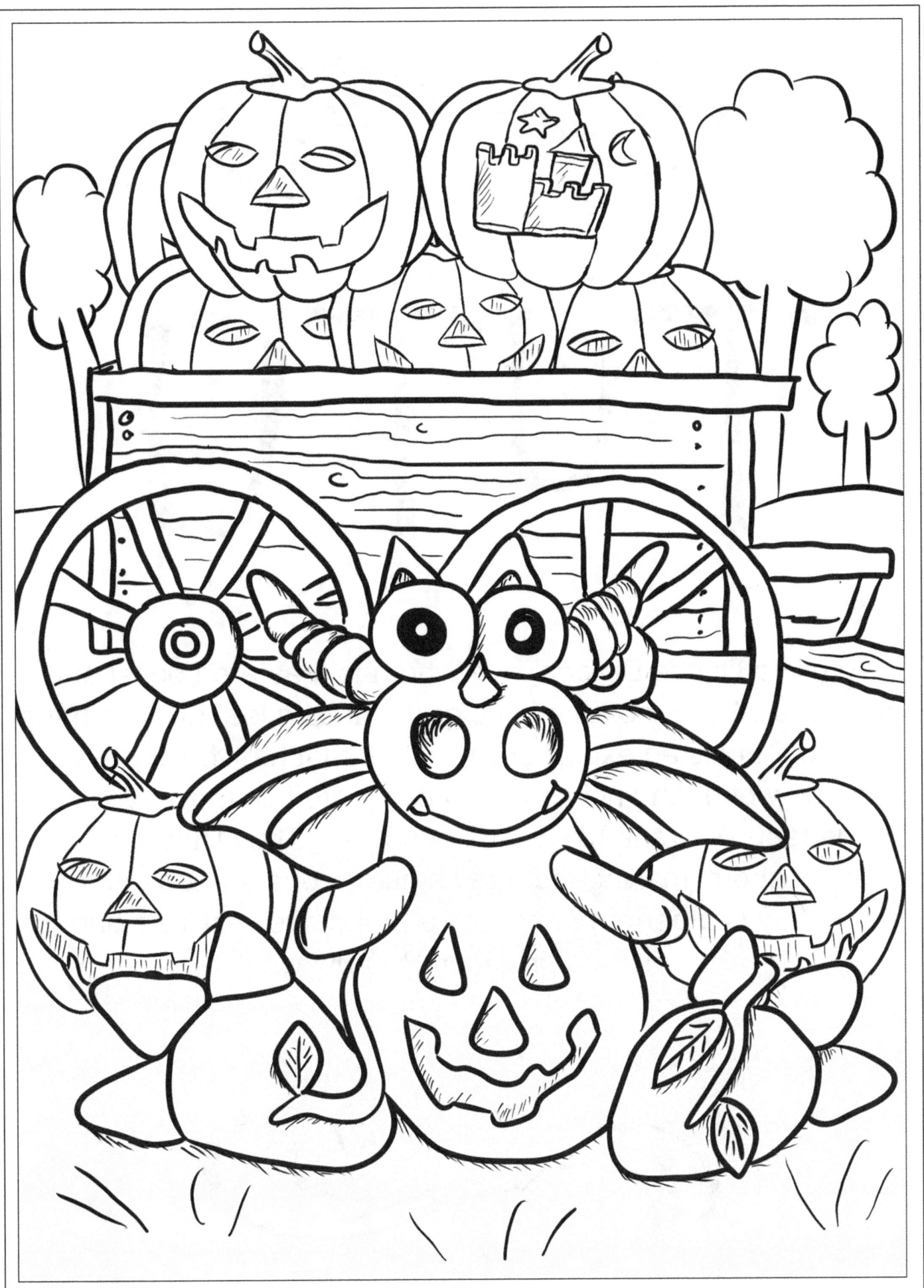

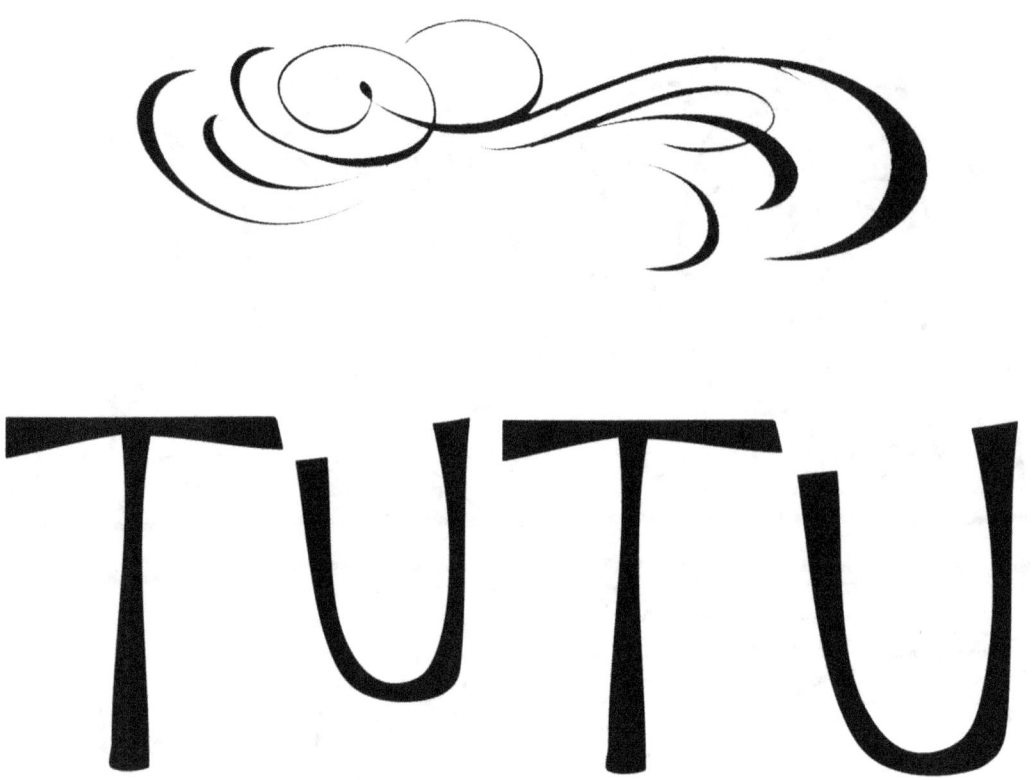

TUTU

Tutu is a Dance Dragon, one who has mastered ballet and cuteness all at once. She is as graceful as a leaf twirling in the wind. Tutu is an expert at pirouettes that has the average person wondering how she can complete this move with her large feet. Why she has wings of course! They lift her as she spins about, making the most adventurous dragons dizzy. Every day is a performance for Tutu and she is still waiting for her big break on Broadway.

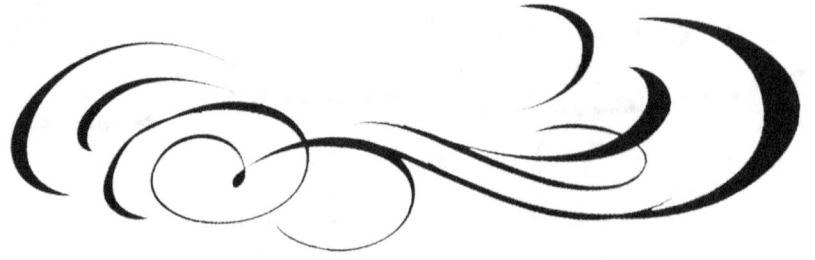

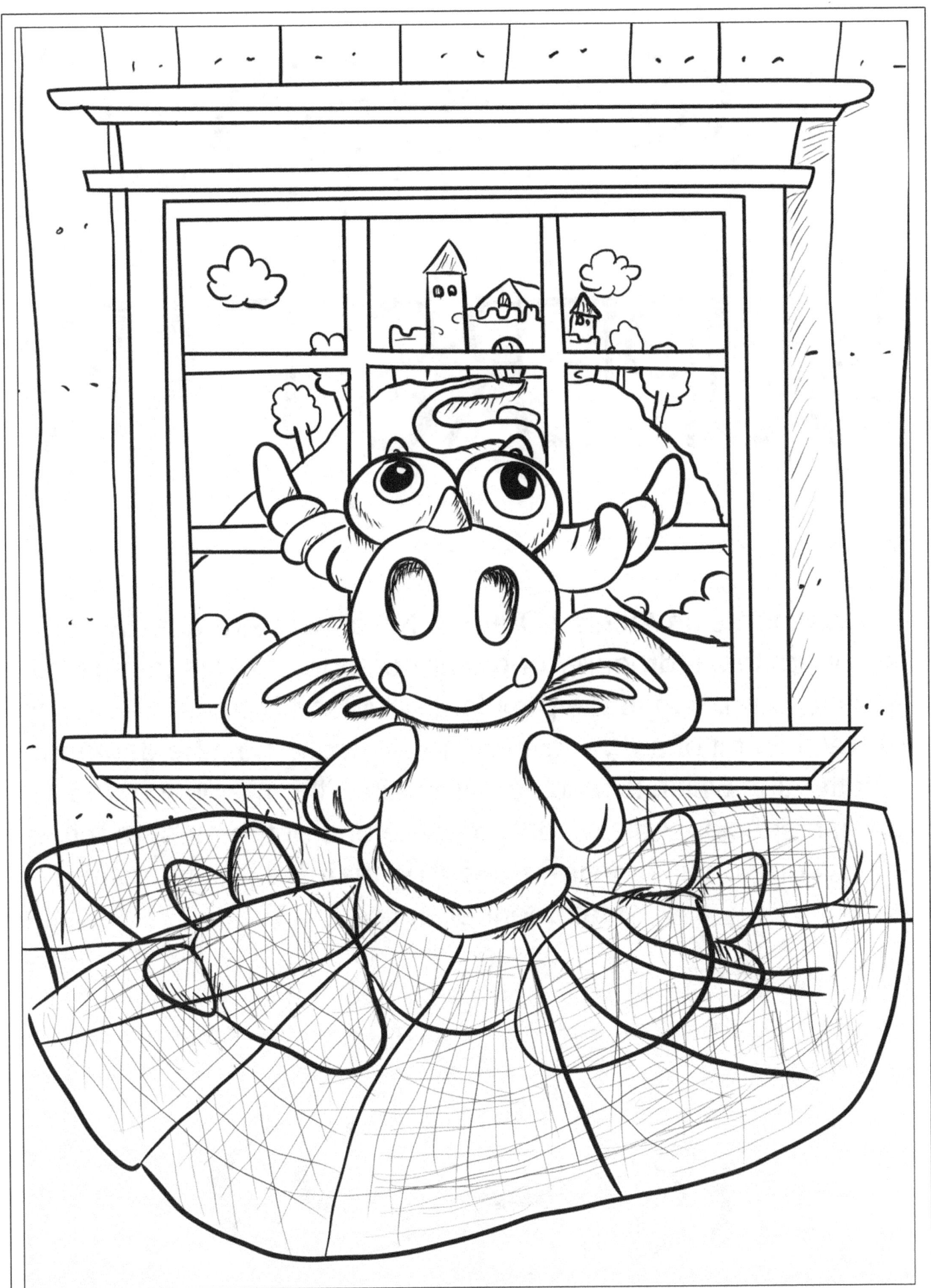

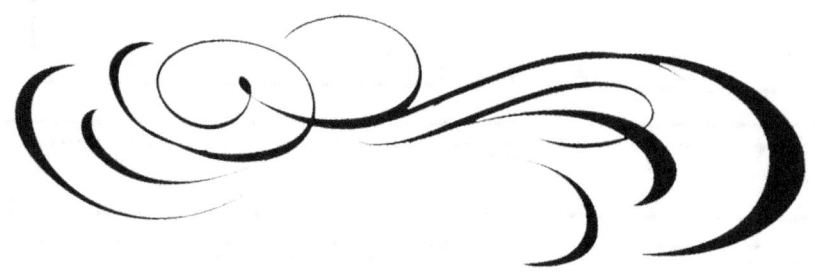

SUPERSTAR

Superstar is an Attitude Dragon. No one knows exactly the history of these dragons' origin or heritage, but it is thought to be a close relation to the popular Hollywood Dragon. Superstar herself is a bit of a diva; glittery and dressed up, she demands attention which is much different than the majority of the dragon species. Attitude dragons are one of the most reactive of all dragons, sometimes showing their fire just to make a statement or noticed.

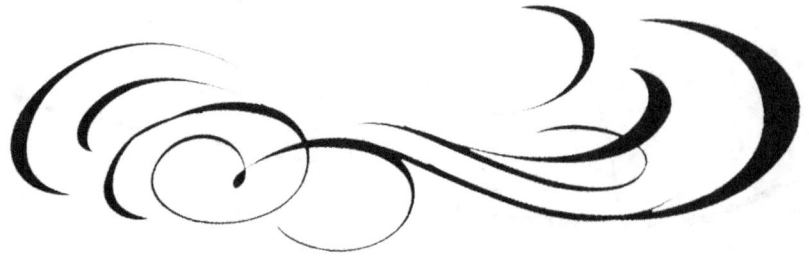

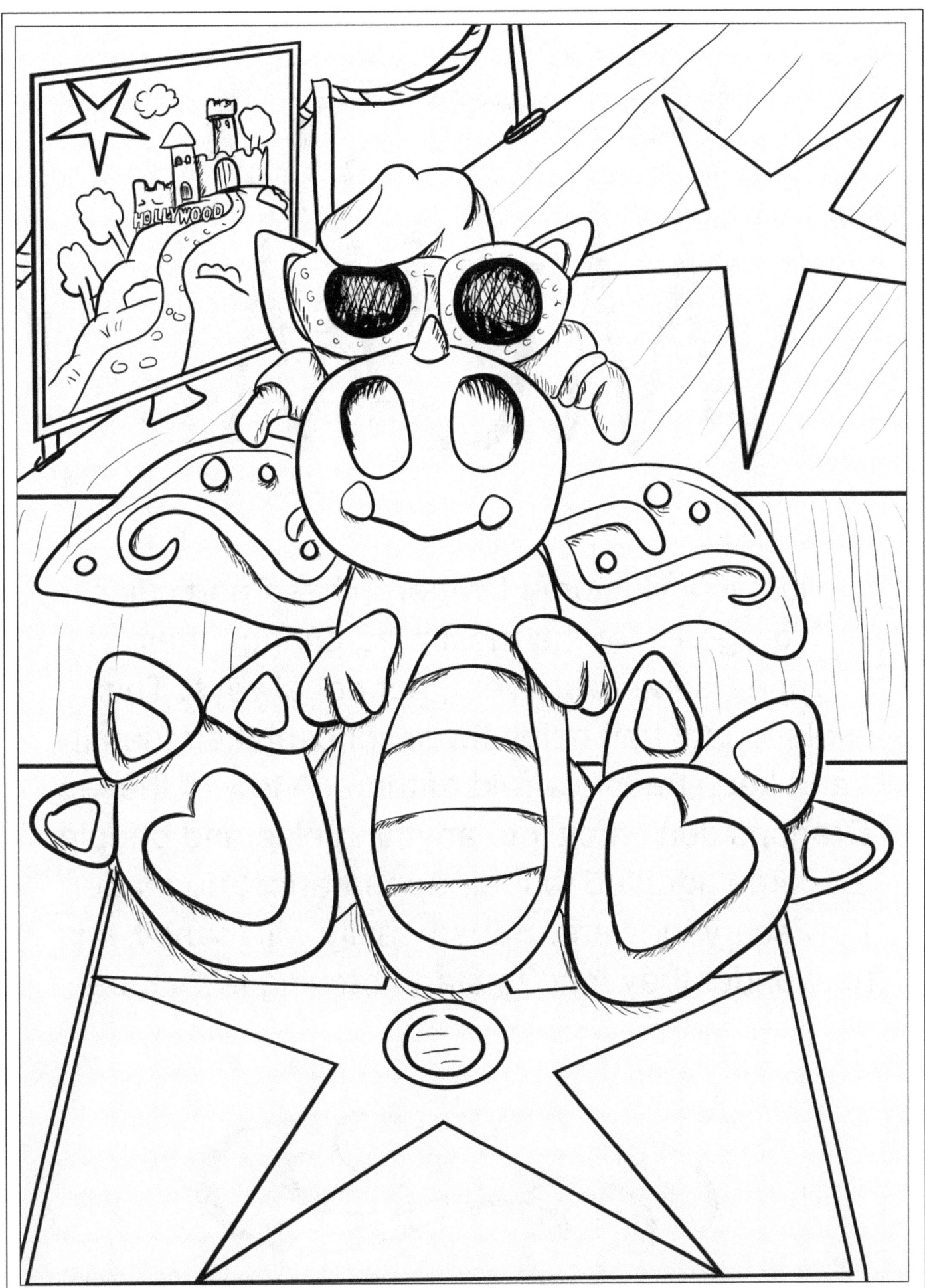

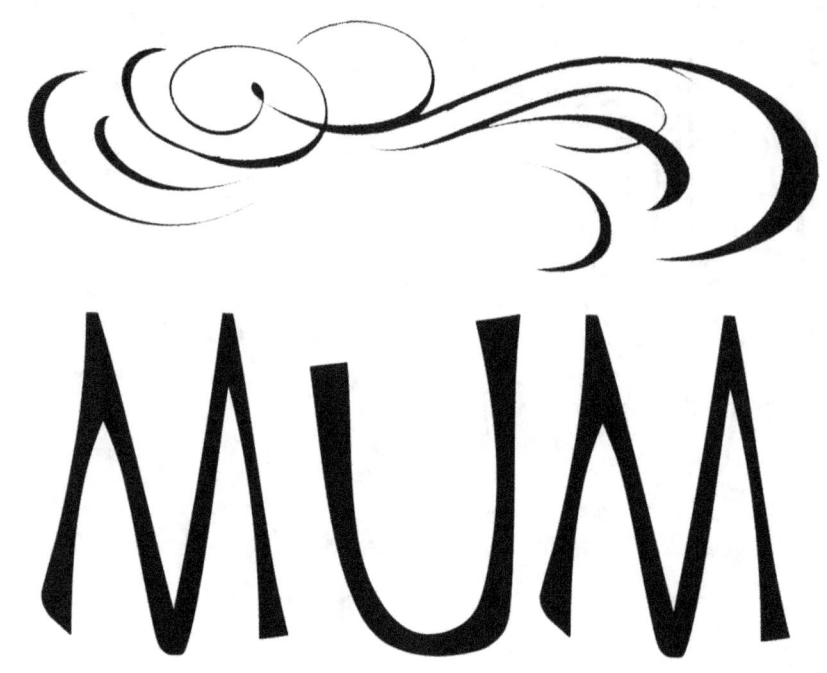

MUM

Mum is a Costume Dragon. These particular dragons, for the most part, change their appearance every year, but not always. This evolutionary trait helps them conceal their identity and keep people afraid of them. A few of these Dragons don't molt into anything else and people become adapted to their appearance, no matter how scary they are. Bribed easily with candy, it is no wonder they tend to start hatching in October.

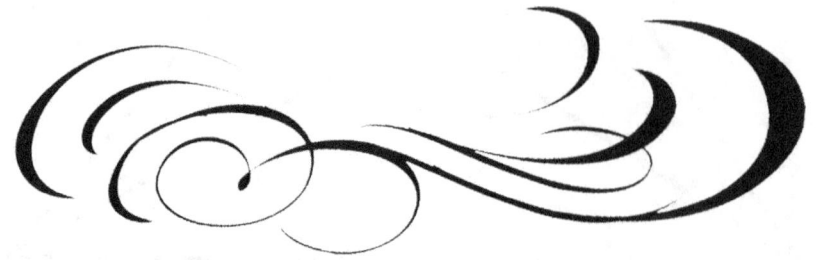

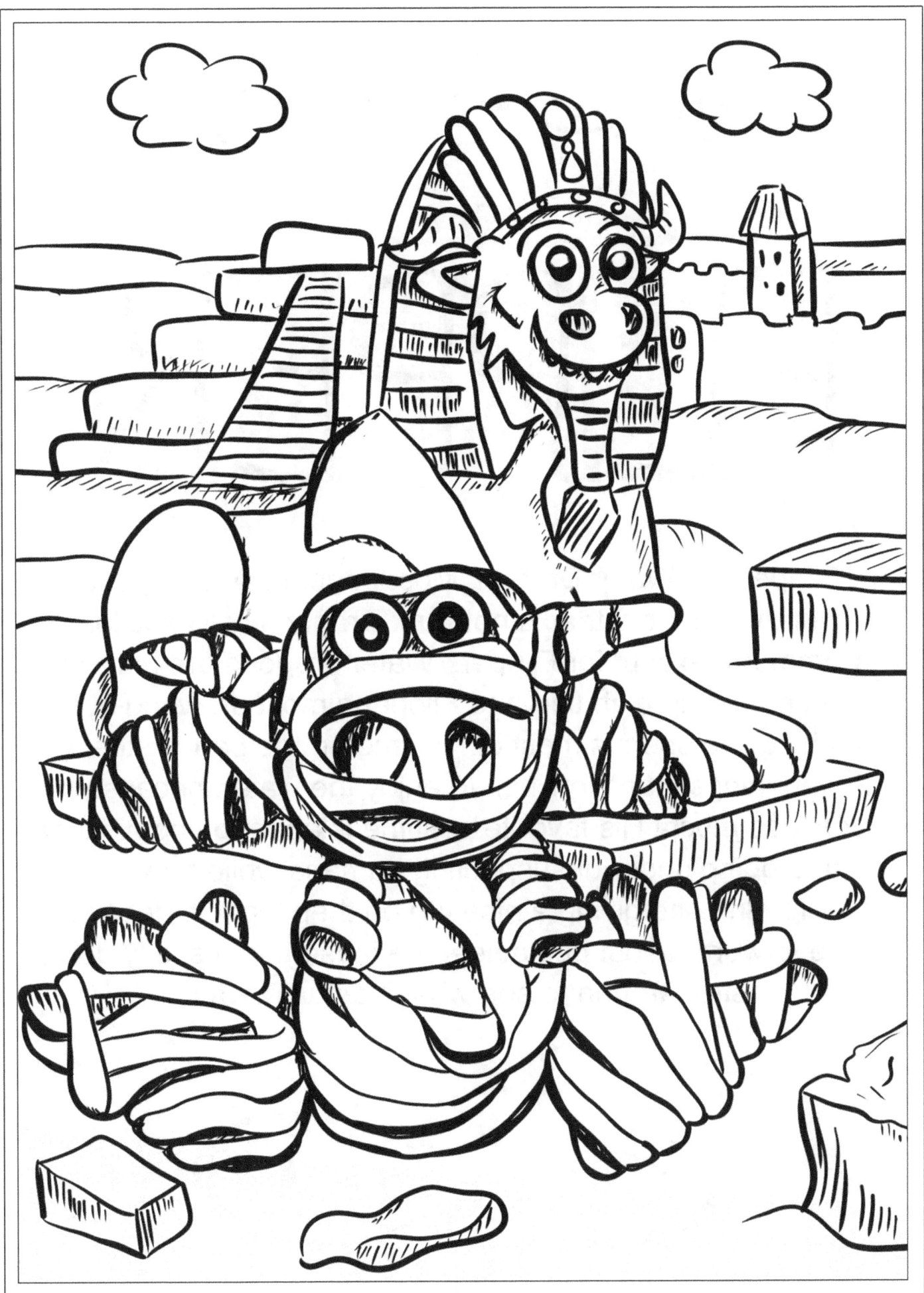

FLIPPER

Flipper is a Water Dragon. Most people think dragons cannot swim, but that is not true. Dragons are excellent swimmers- except for Flipper. Water dragons are born on the sand during high tide and Flipper almost drowned at his hatching. He spends most of his time on the beach stealing human things that allow him to enjoy the water, because he loves it so much! His favorite pastime is abandoning his tube and going under unsuspecting humans while they are swimming and giving a nice tug on their leg. He doesn't have to worry about being seen because they usually don't stick around to see what it actually was.

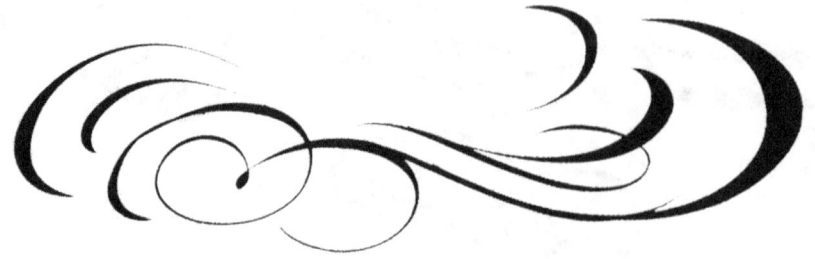

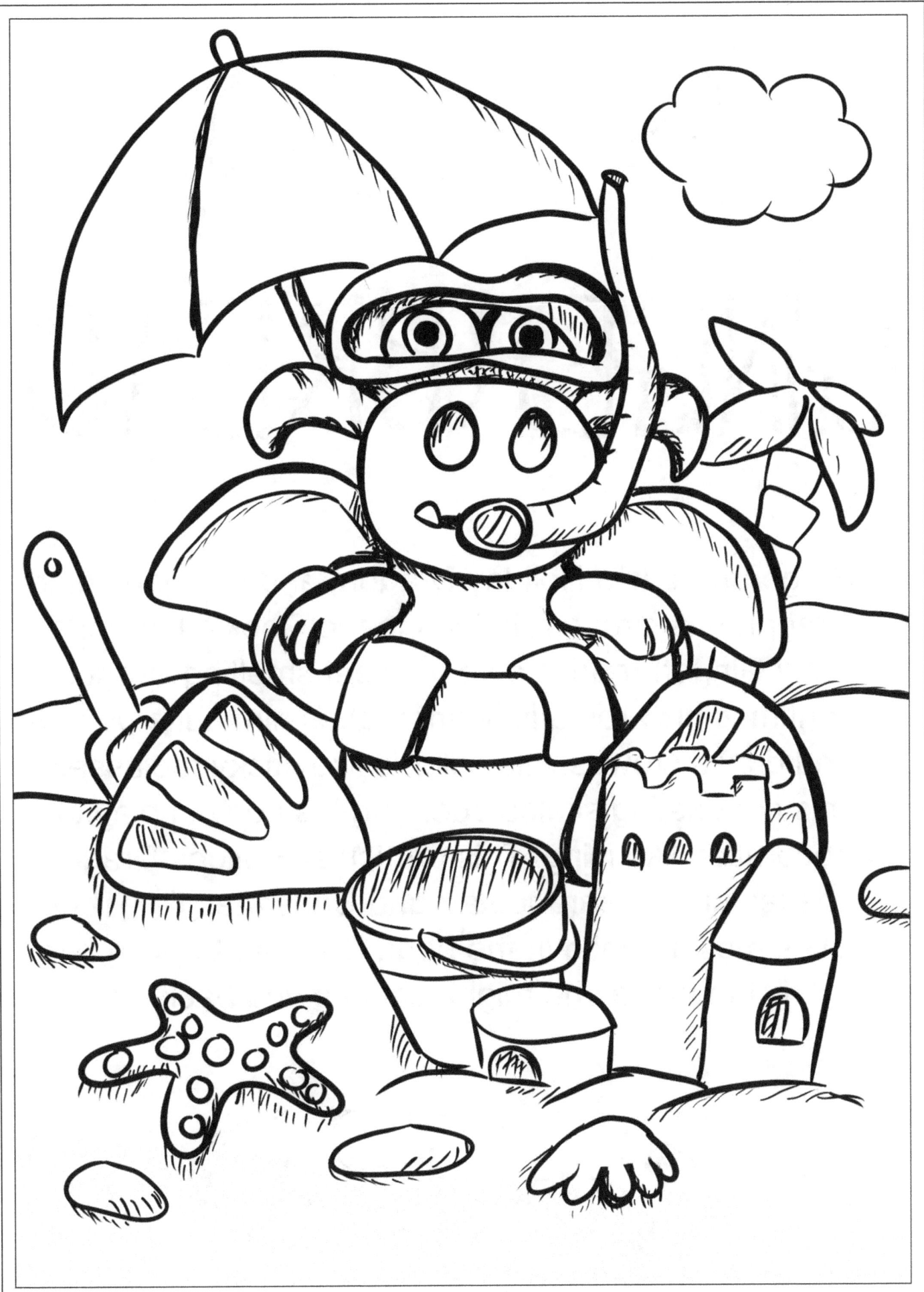

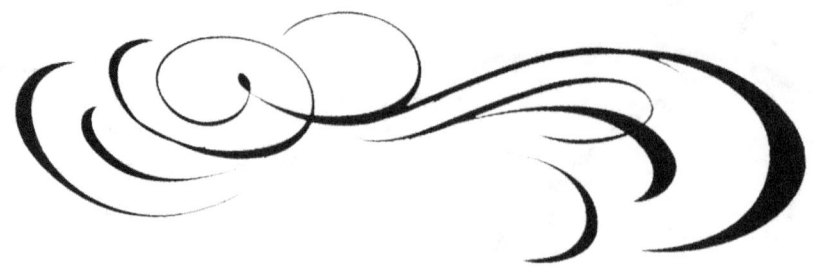

GINGERBREAD

Gingerbread is a Holiday Dragon, and this particular Dragon has strong relations to the Cookie Dragons. Now Gingerbread is a very sweet smelling Dragon, oftentimes his aromatic scent makes him quite popular and draws crowds. His color is like sticky molasses, his contrasting scales adorning his body in playful decoration like icing. This particular Holiday Dragon makes his appearance around Christmas time, but loves most to bake in the heat. Don't try to taste him though, as he might just bite you back.

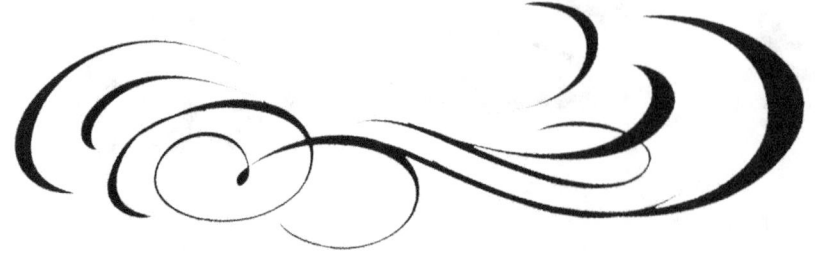

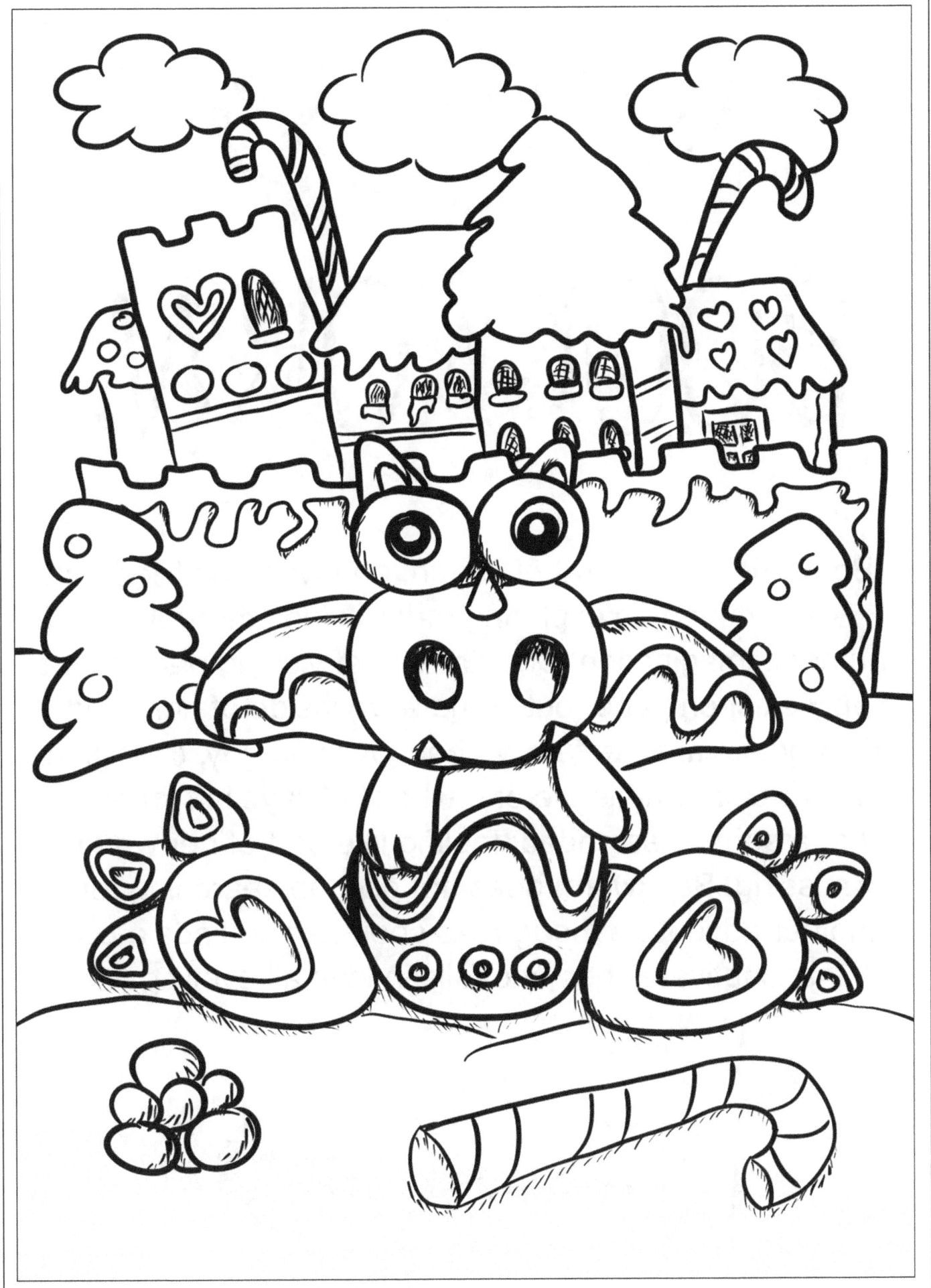

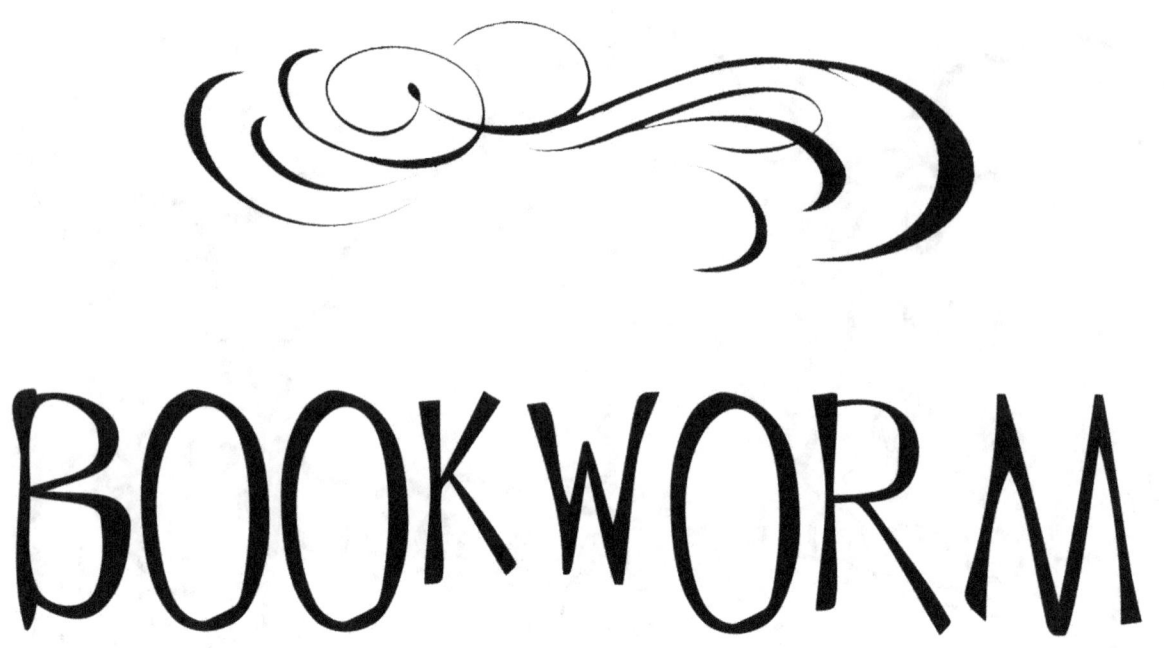

BOOKWORM

Bookworm is a Library Dragon, one who has filled her days curled up exploring other worlds through an author's imagination. She dreams of visiting places that only exist on paper but come alive inside of her mind. Characters are like family; their joy is her joy, their pain is her pain. She is the one who is always left longing after a series has ended; feeling like part of her world is missing. Bookworm does not give up searching for another adventure though. As soon as she finds a book that captivates her, she falls in love all over again.

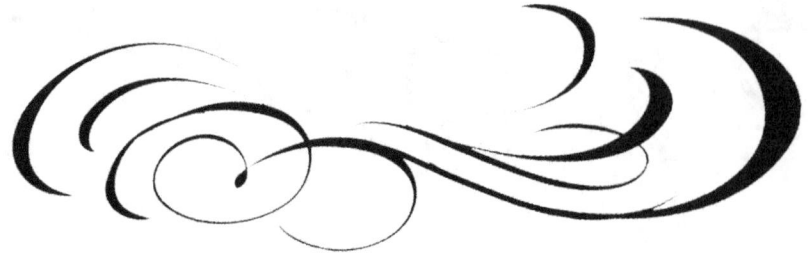

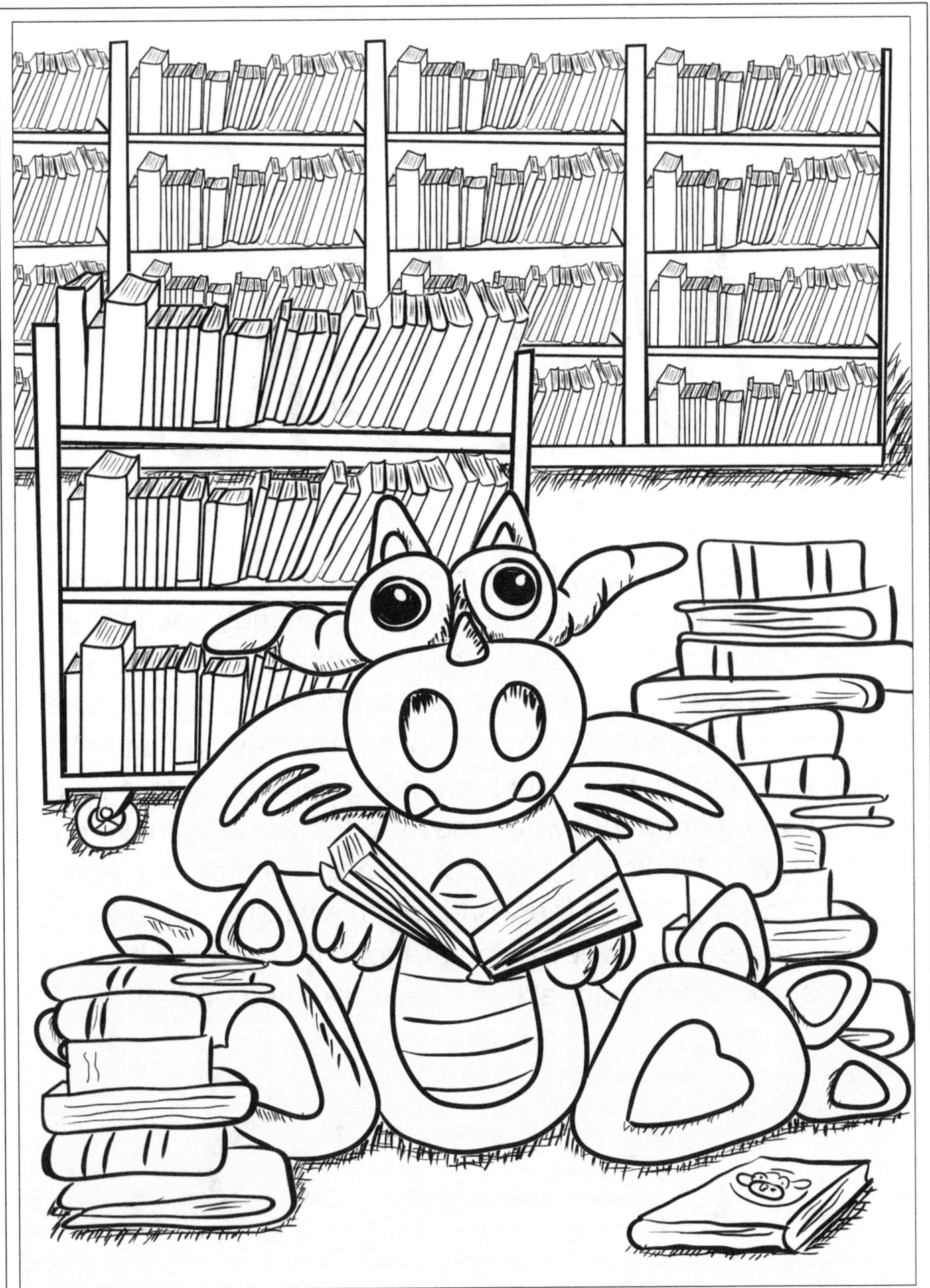

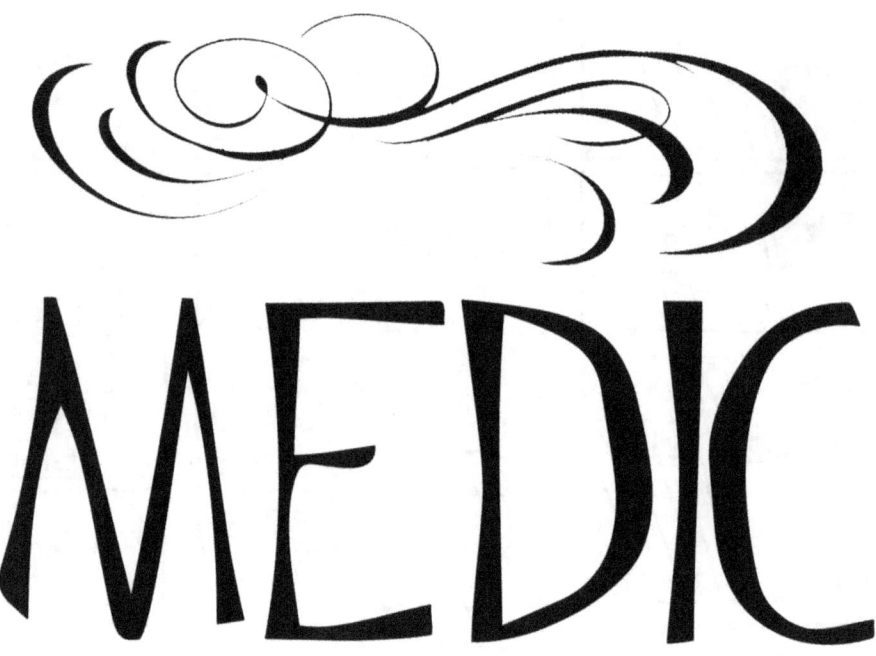

MEDIC

Medic is a Caretaker Dragon, one who has fulfilled their lifelong dream of being a nurse, now that they have been assigned to someone who has become ill with a nasty disease. As a Caretaker Dragon, Medic will be responsible for caring for them as the patient overcomes any and all obstacles. Medic will nurture whenever their body fails them and carry them about when they are too weak to move on their own. Medic will also provide positive thoughts and allow them to travel the world with his wings. Caretaker Dragons also are sweet loving dragons that also nibble and show affection to take the patient's mind off pain.

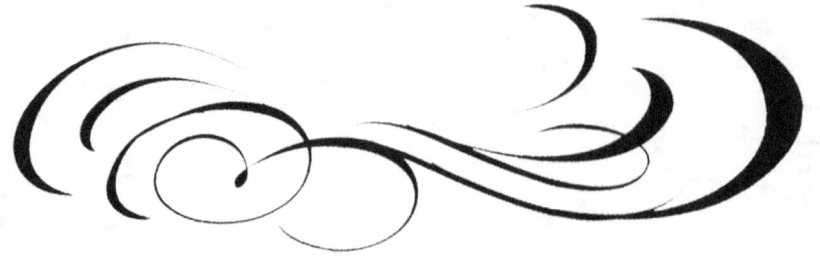

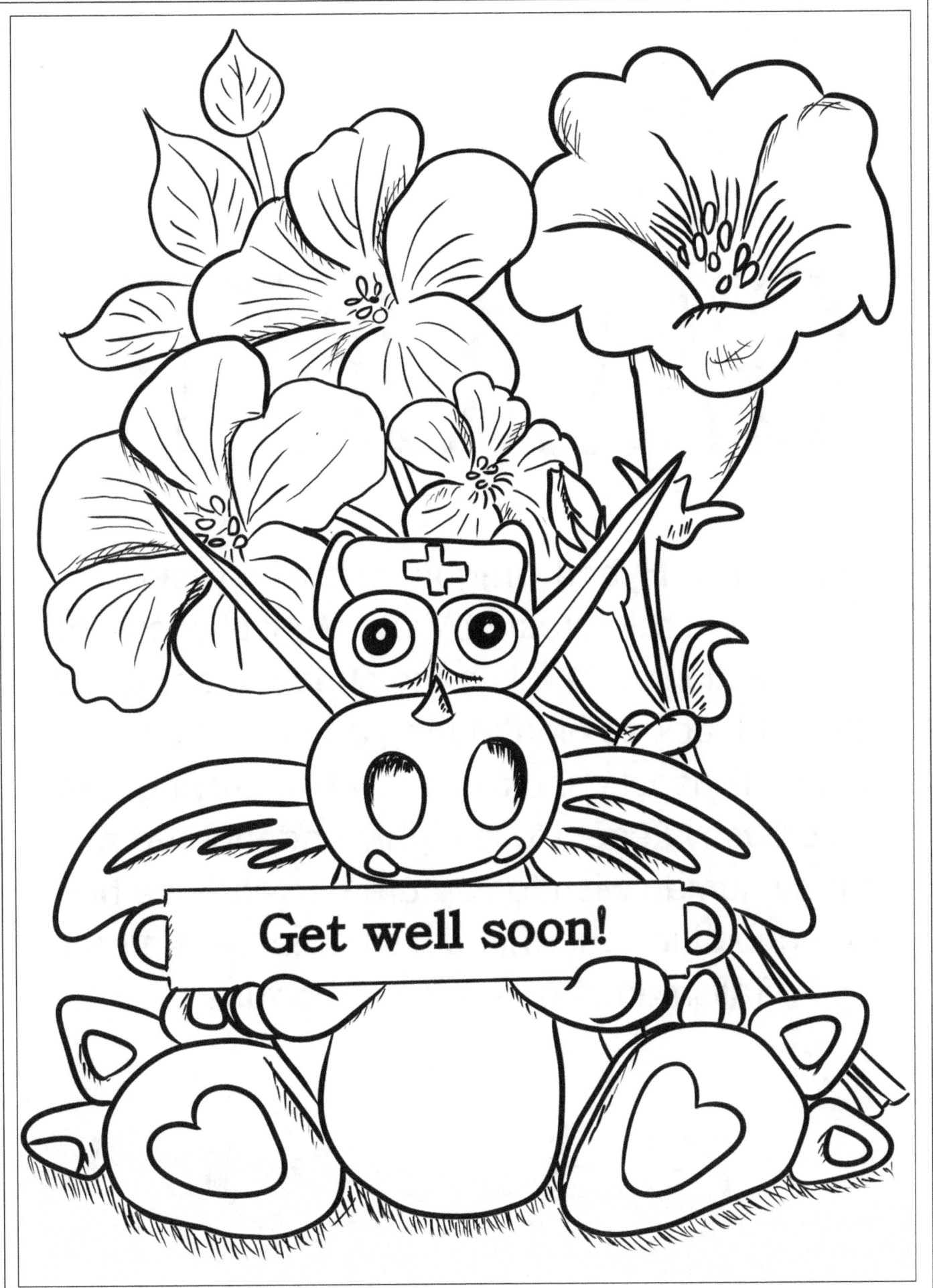

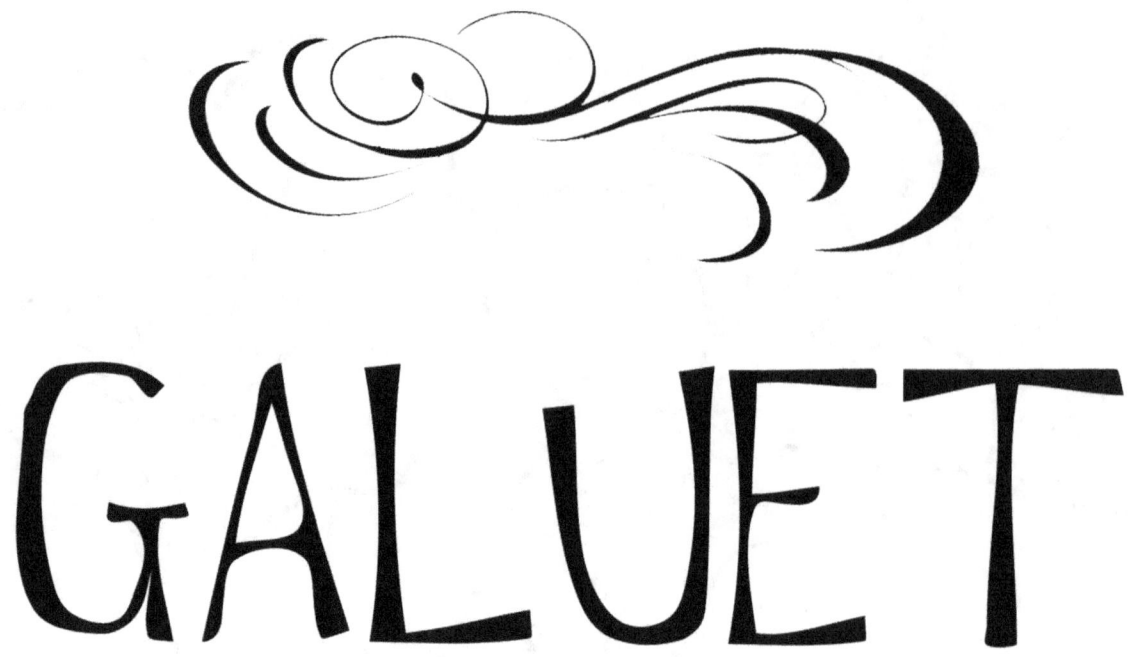

GALUET

Galuet is a Hybrid Dragon, one who resides in the tropical rainforest of Vran. Densely covered in vegetation that makes the shady undergrowth almost black as night during daytime, he preys on small insects and rodents while staying near his bushy keep. He is highly endangered as many human wish to capture him and use him as a good luck charm, as his name translates to "Talisman of a Thousand Fortunes".

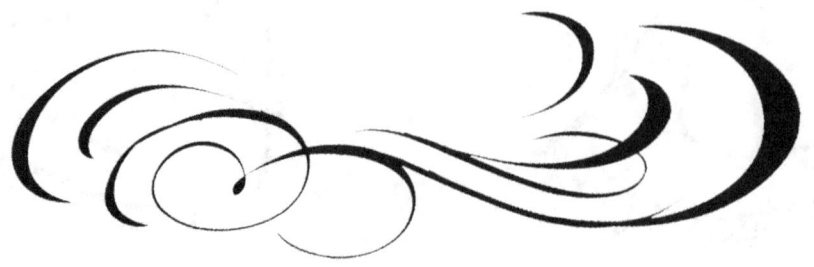

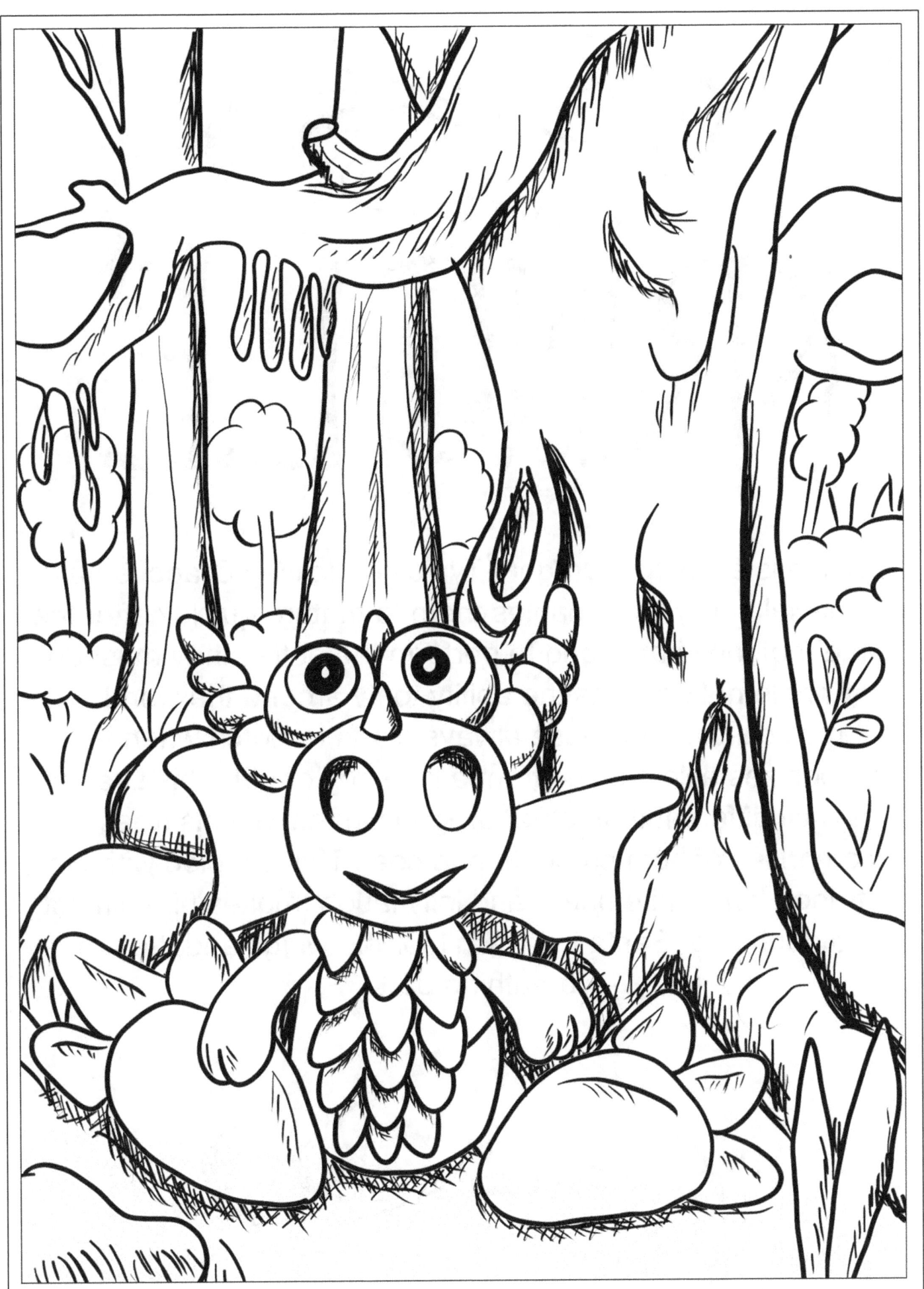

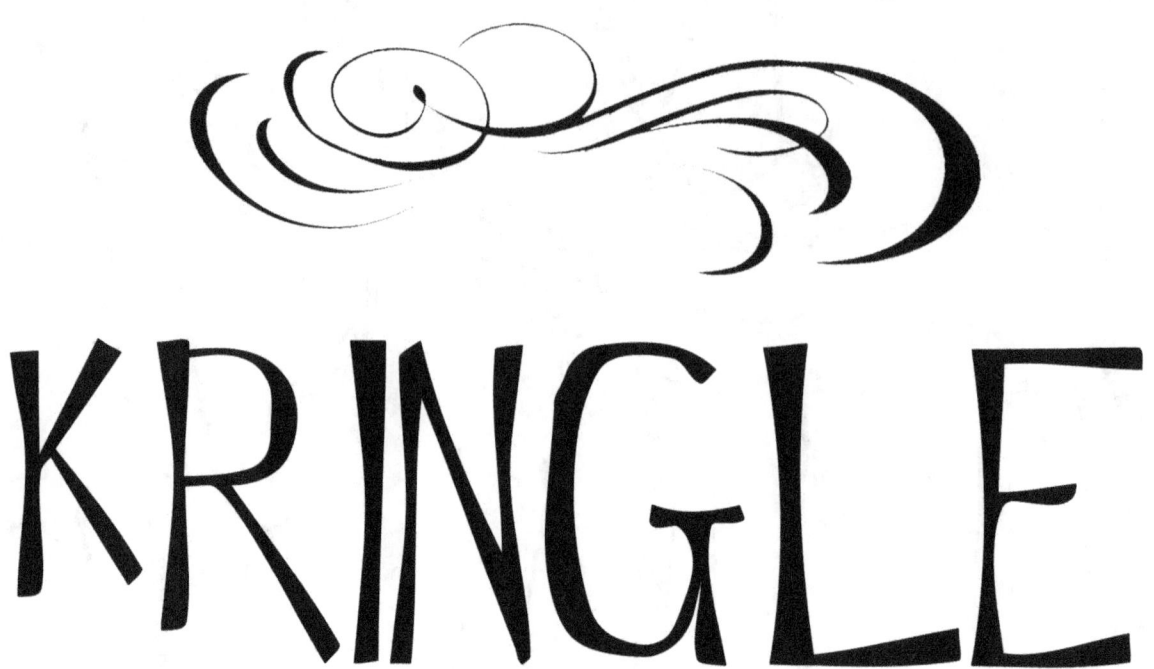

KRINGLE

Kringle is a Holiday Dragon. Typically Holiday Dragons have a special ability that enables them to mature quickly after the time that they hatch and to perform the duties they must do. Kringle not only has the ability to fly around the world in magical time, his nose always starts to twitch when he recognizes a lie coming from a little boy or girl. This Dragon is a bit different than other dragons in the fact his treasure comprises of both presents and coal. This coupled with his strange long white beard and jolly laugh, makes him almost a double for Santa if it wasn't for the wings and the fire breathing part.

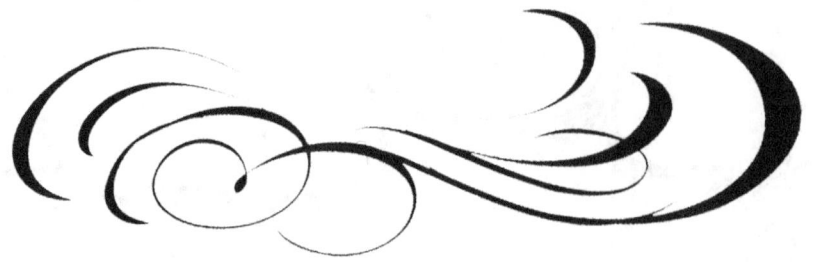

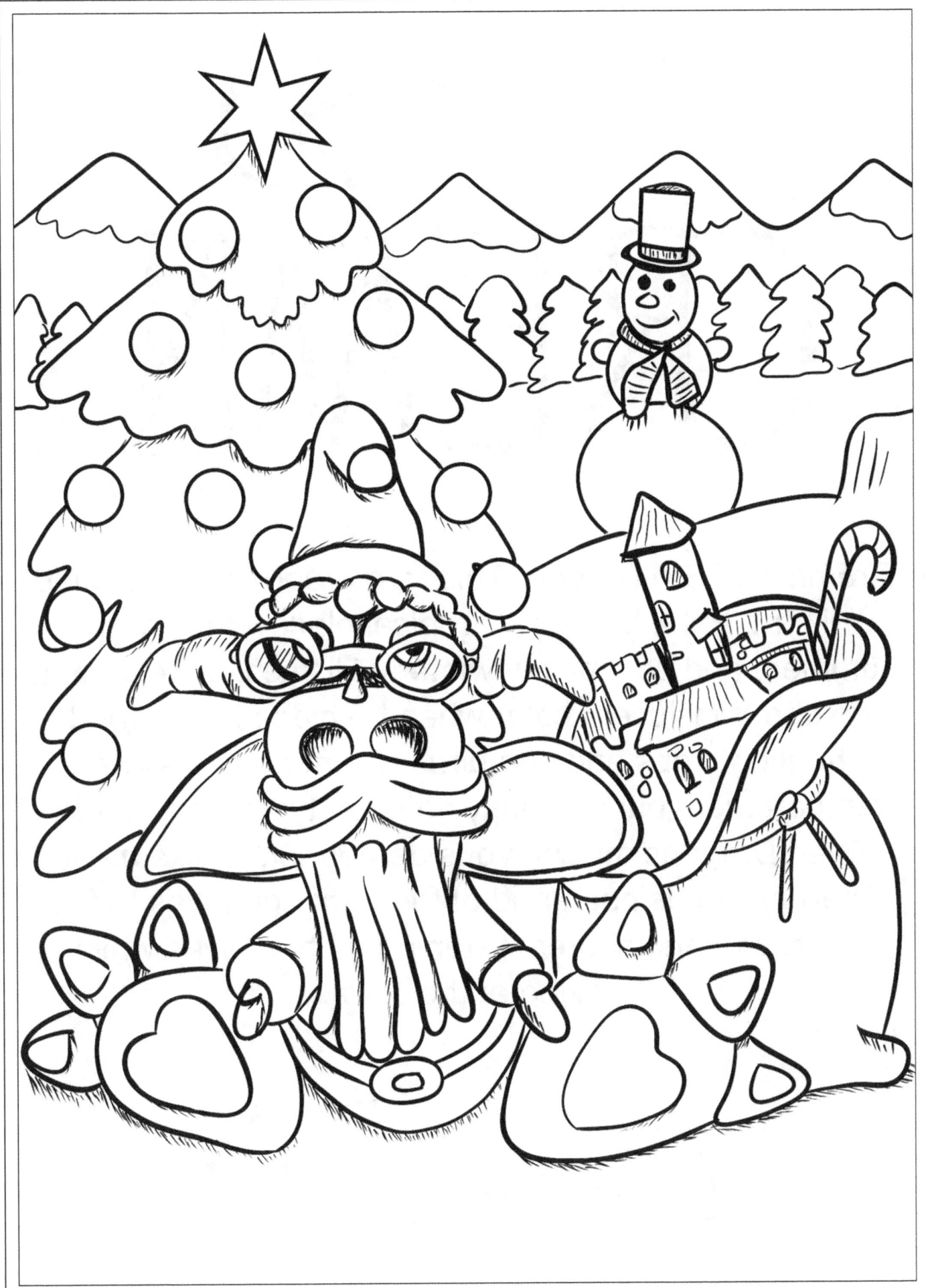

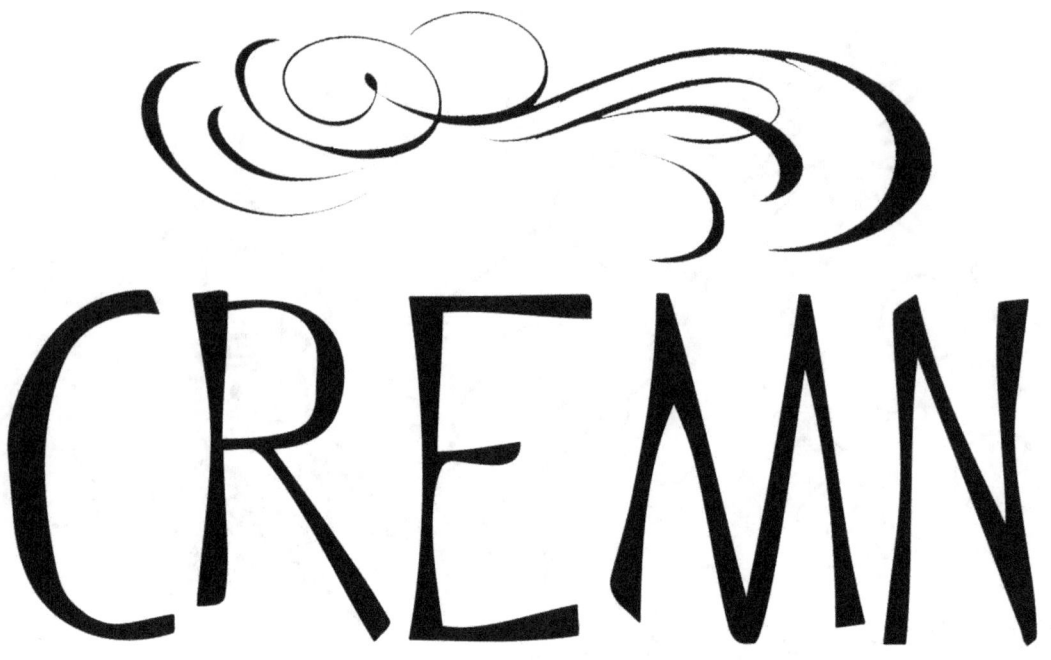

CREMN

Cremn is a Fire Dragon. This rare dragon was hatched in the Pehx Islands, a tropical place with warm summers and cool balmy winters. His scales become a golden translucent color when he hides in the sand, hunting crabs and sea birds. Cremn has a sweet temperament but a spunky attitude, typical of the Fire Eyed Dragons mischievous demeanor. Unlike most Dragons, he is not afraid of the dark and loves to fall asleep on the shores, listening to the waves while gazing at the stars.

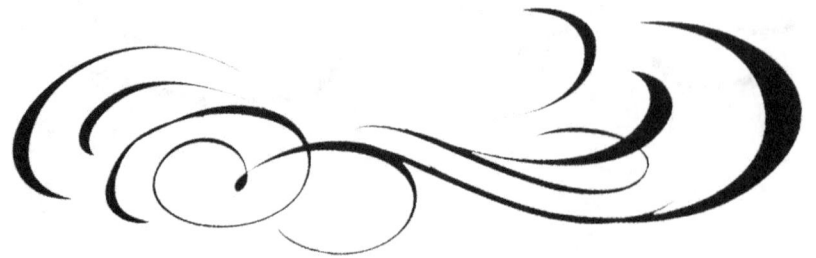

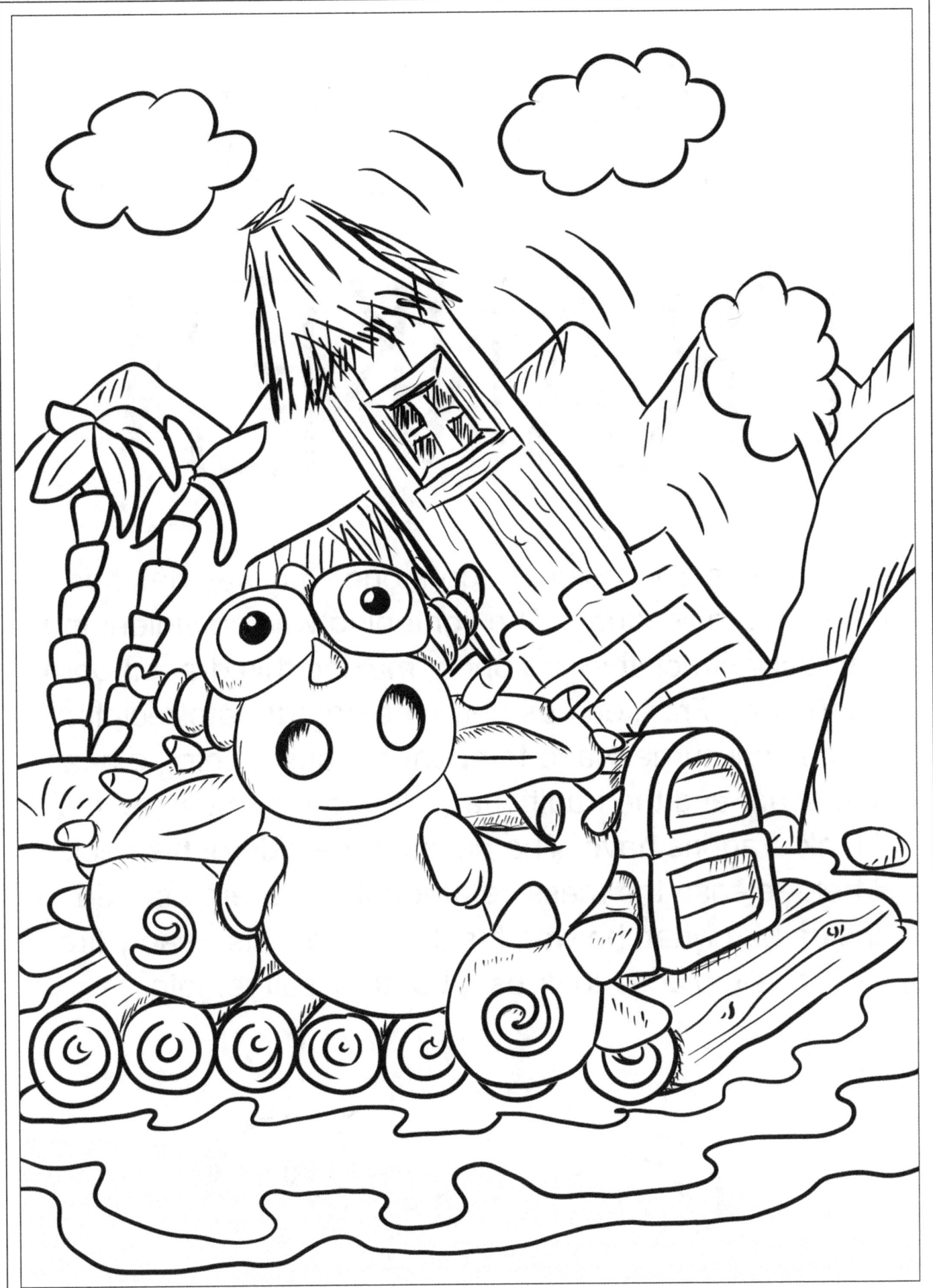

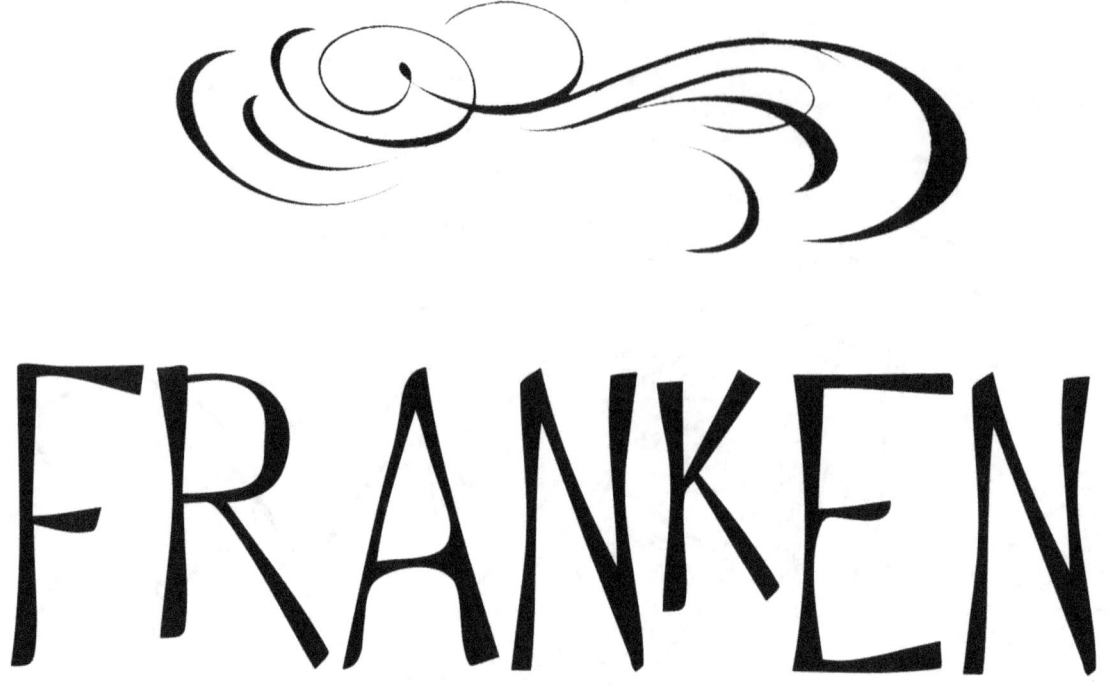

FRANKEN

Franken is a Monster Dragon, one who was hatched during a terrible storm. The lightening was so violent that it actually struck the egg open, making this dragon born premature. Franken has been the unfortunate recipient of medical surgery and tampering, causing him to bear the scars and the traditional coloring that most people think dragons have. The bolts on the side of his neck help release the massive amounts of energy stored inside him when he was first born. Now his deadly fire has replaced their use, but they still remain.

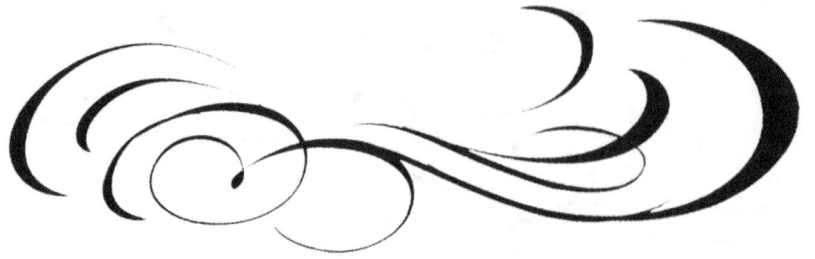

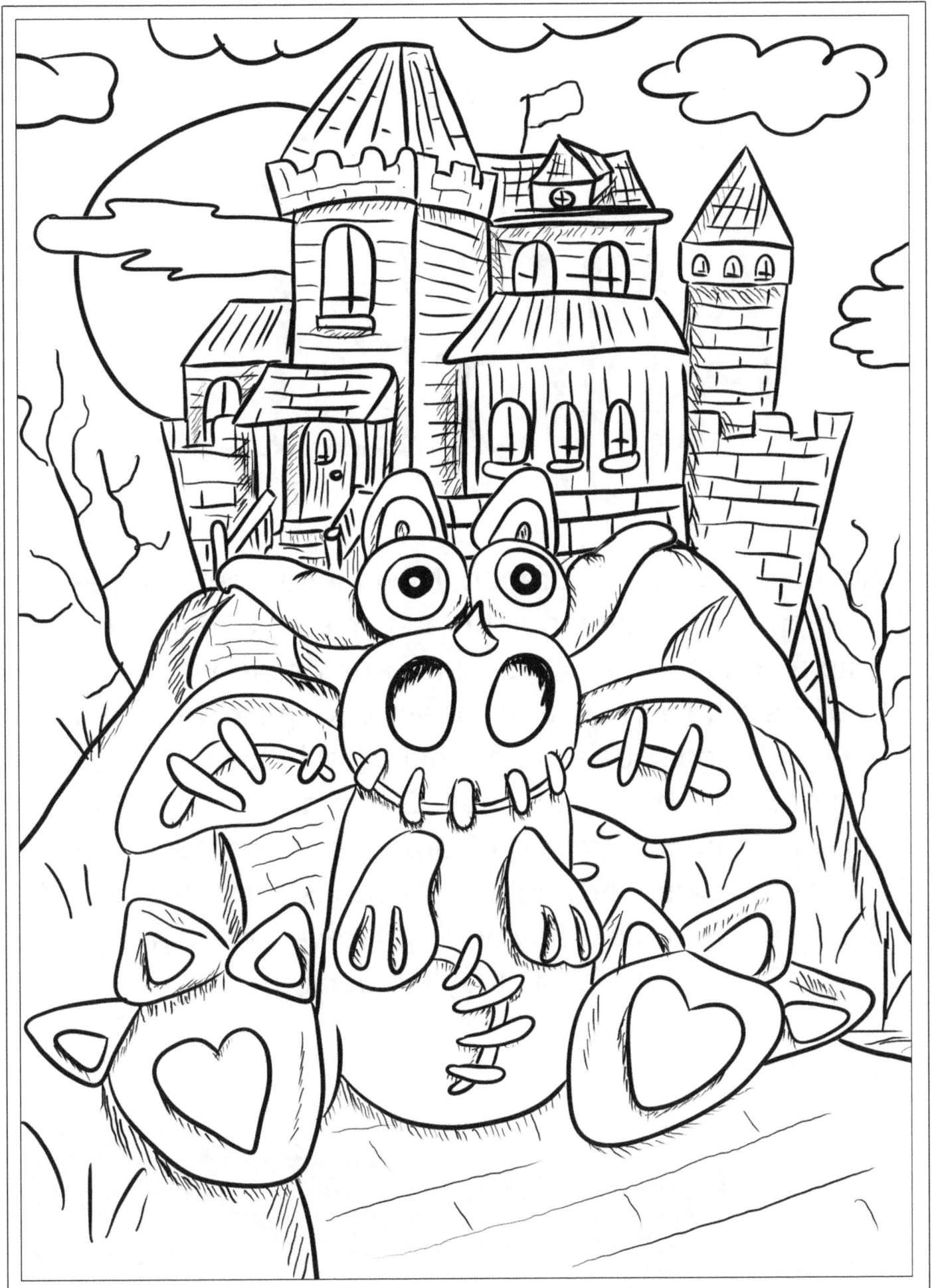

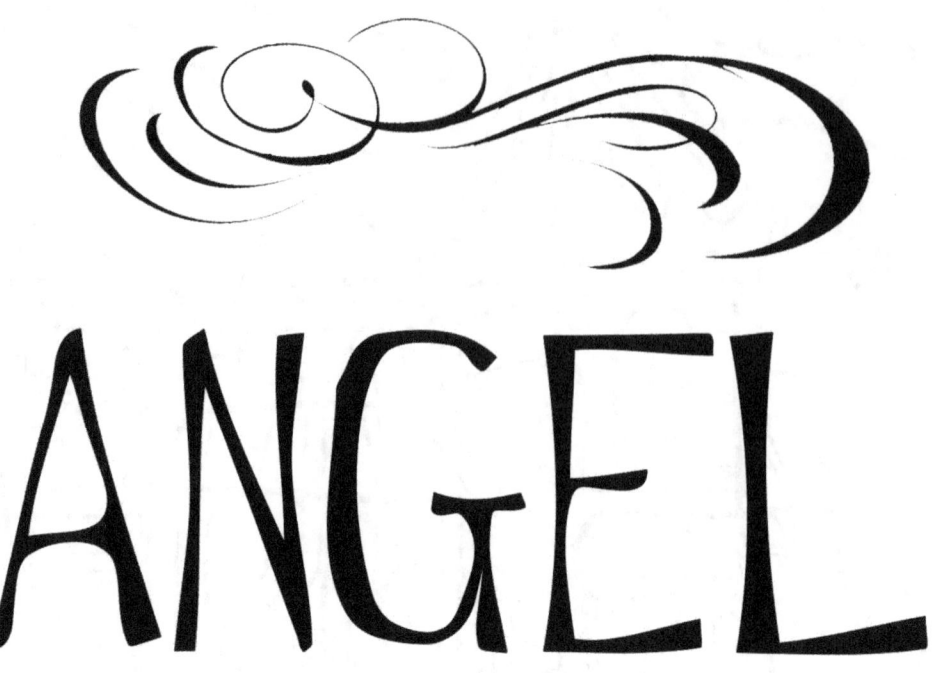

ANGEL

Angel is a Guardian Dragon. Now these Dragons make an appearance on the earth and finish the rest of their life among the deep blue skies and heavenly clouds, free of struggles. Angel has feather wings instead of the typical Dragon scales and a halo that helps them be in tuned with their loved ones. Guardian Dragons are known to be the bravest of Dragons as they deal with many obstacles. They fight courageously until the end of their earthly battle. They will live forever watching over their family they left behind.

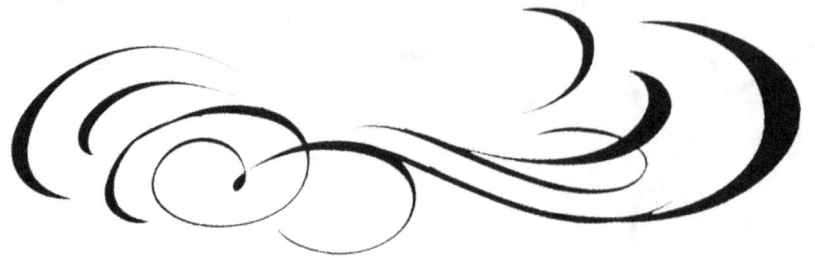

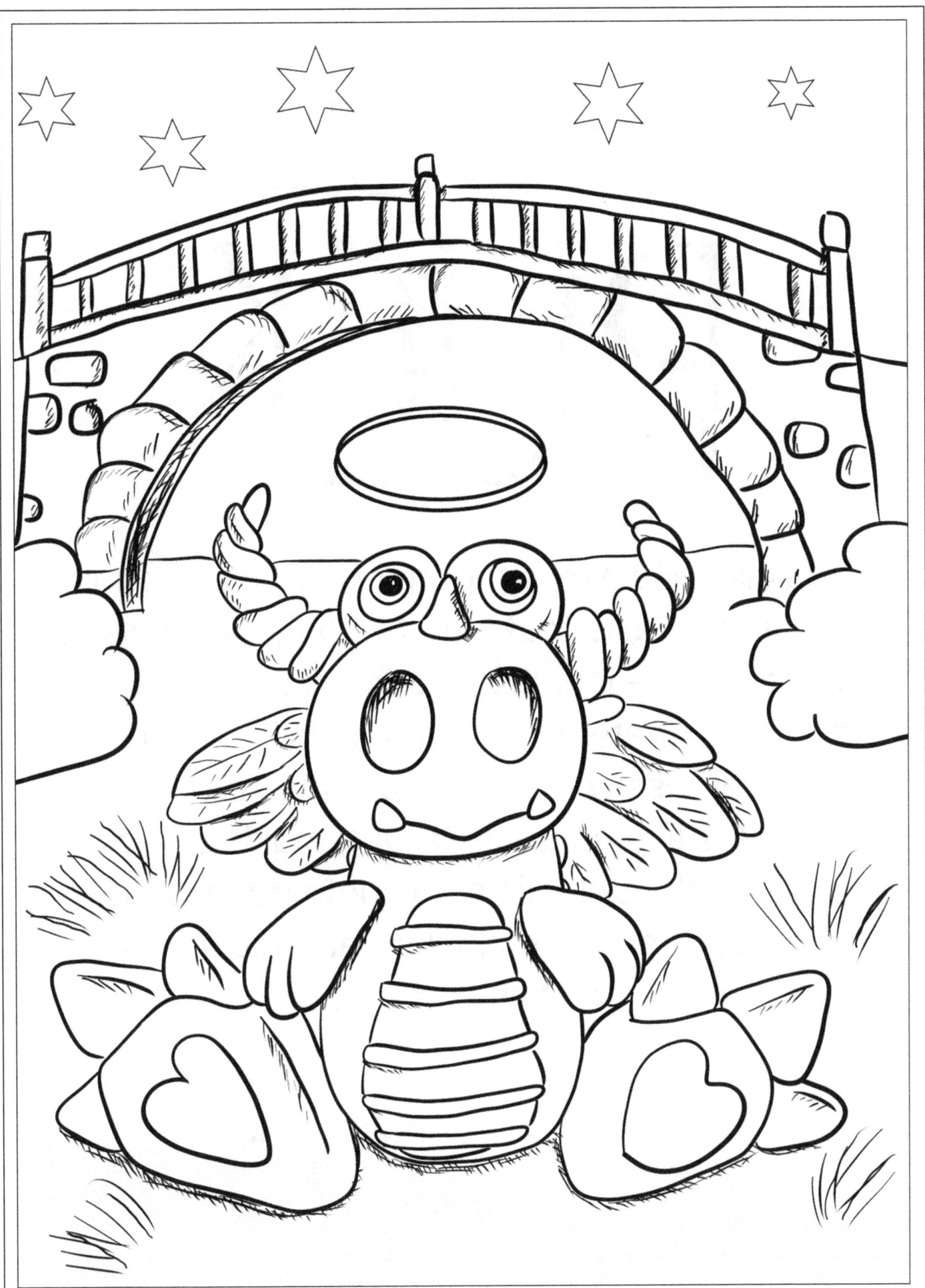

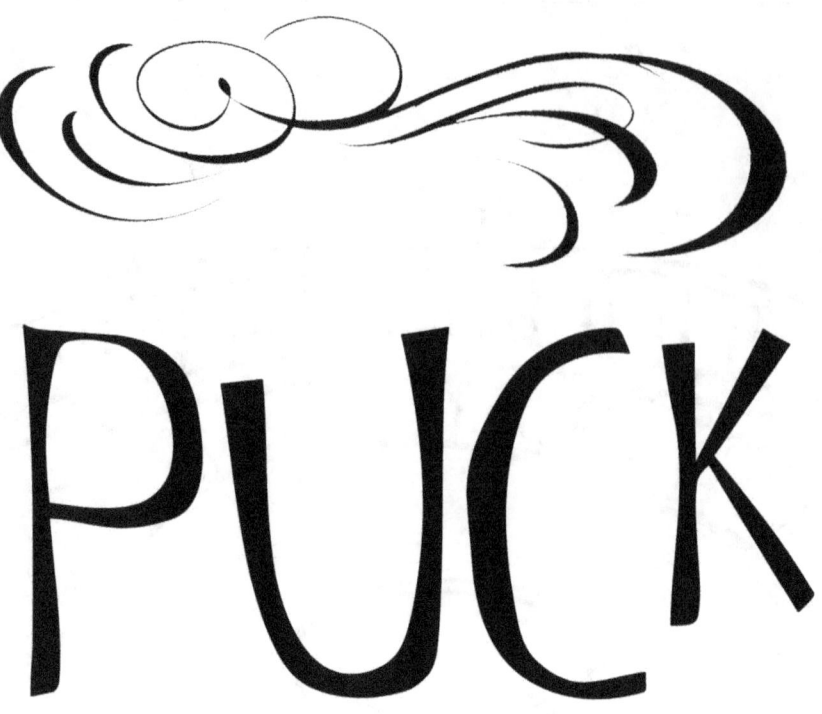

PUCK

Puck is a Hockey Dragon, one that performs unbelievable acts that lead to goals. Rumored to be born on the ice, this Dragon has a glide over the frozen water that is unmatched. His focus and aggressive behavior are overwhelming when it is fixated on its target, making Puck a tough contender. His slap shots travel so fast they can't even be clocked and his favorite position is goalie.

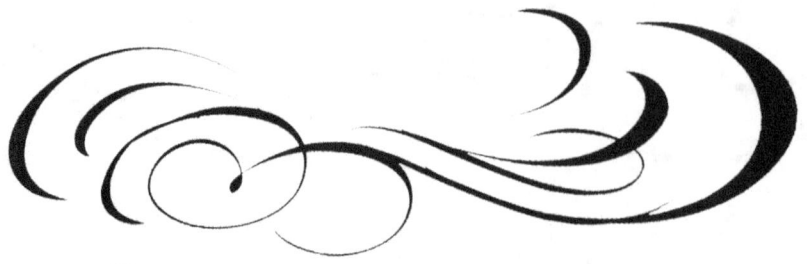

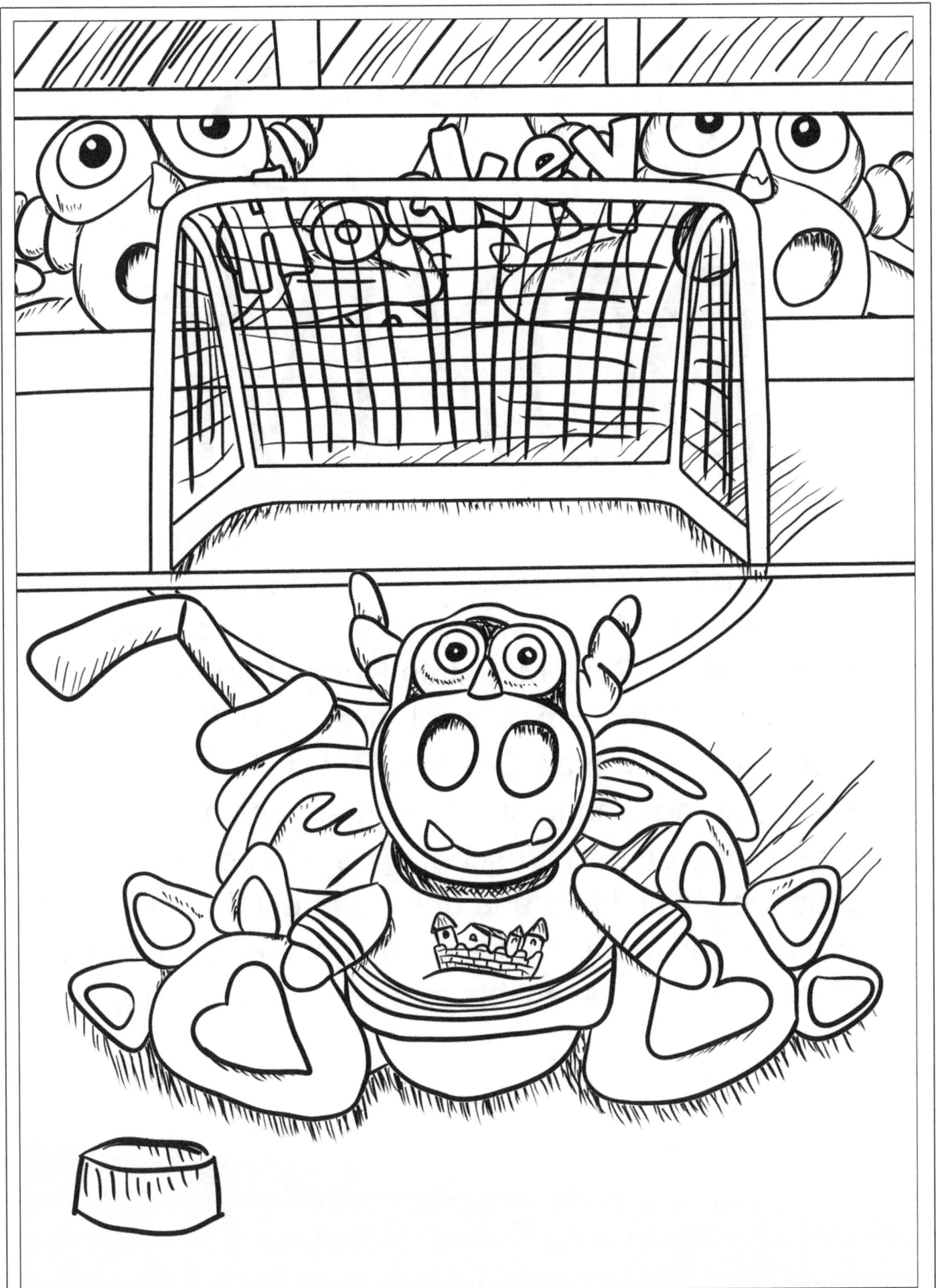

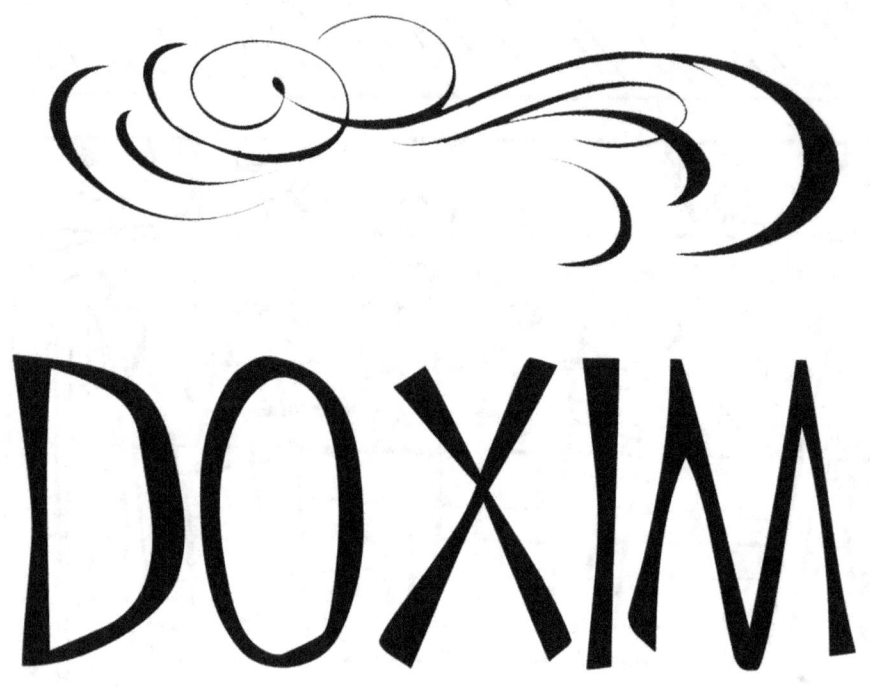

DOXIM

Doxim is an Albino Dragon. These rare dragons can be found in any location, but do prefer the snowy seclusion of the Roks Mountain Range for camouflage purposes. With its main peak over 40,000 ft, Myts Crest it is taller than Everest. This is the place of Doxim's home among clouds and sunshine, the blue sky reflecting on his iridescent eyes and scale tips. He feeds mostly on birds and unfortunately due his rare gene has one of the shortest life spans of the Dragon species as he is susceptible to subtle climate changes.

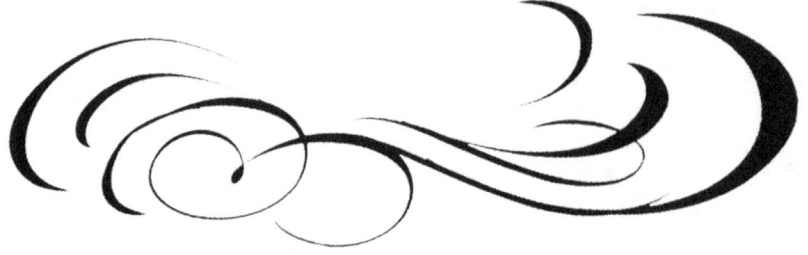

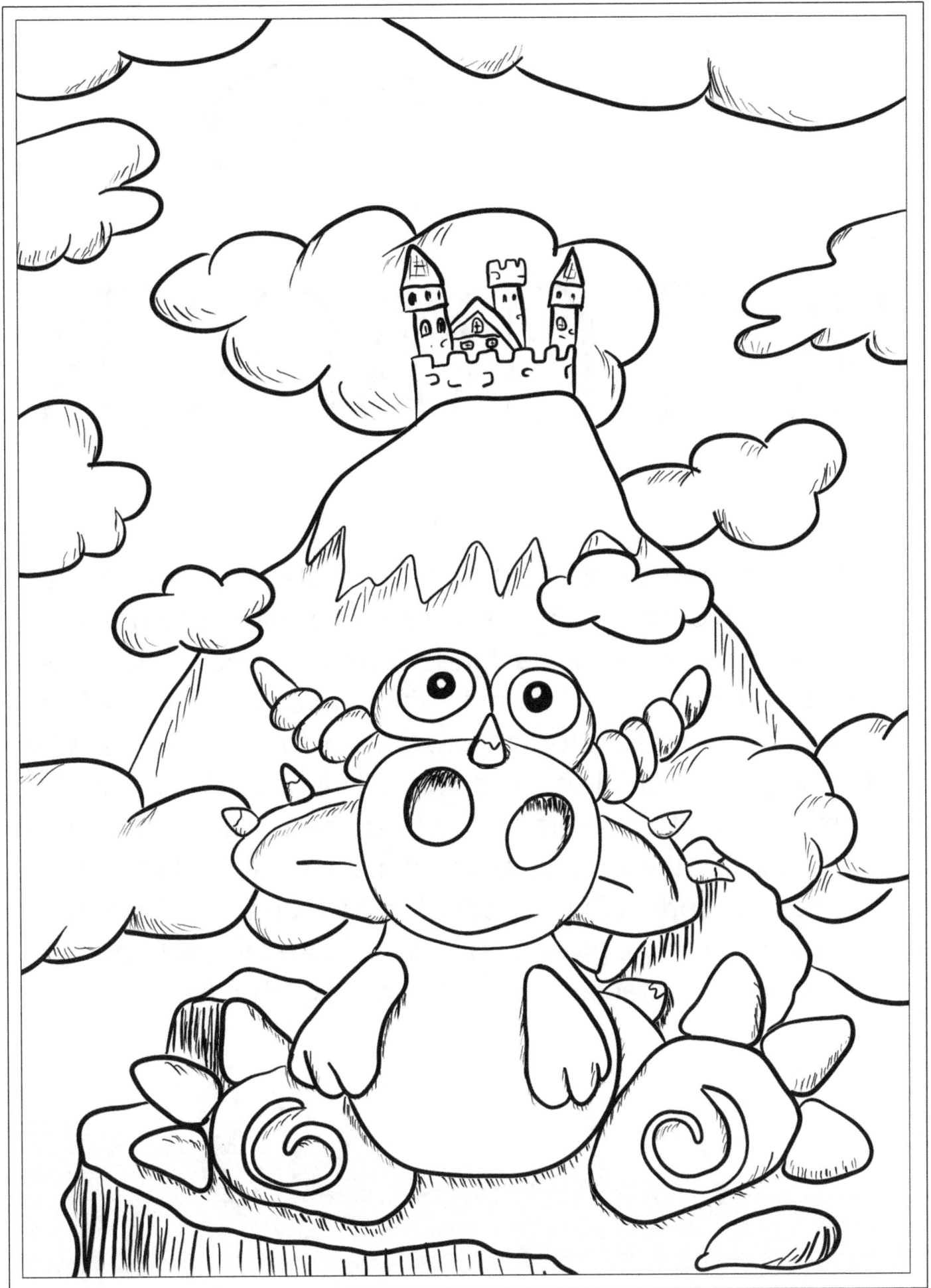

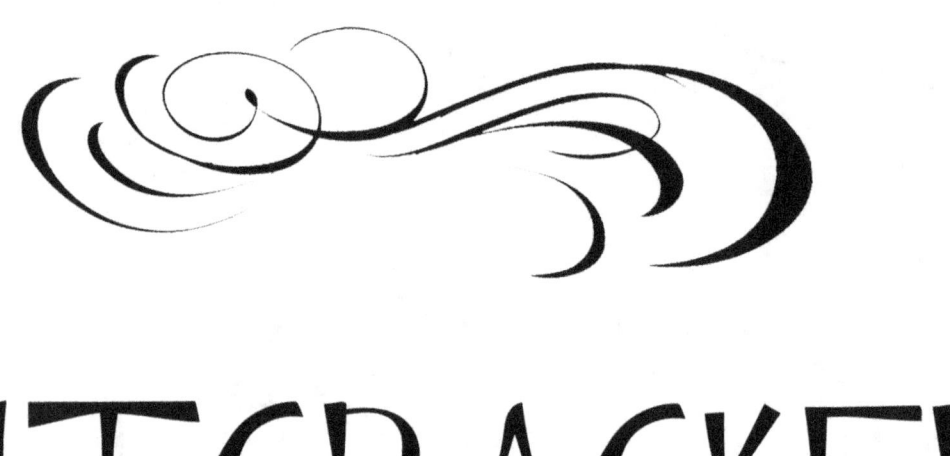

NUTCRACKER

Nutcracker is a Holiday Dragon, one who's lineage dates back prior to the 15th century in Germany. The most powerful and ornately designed Dragons specifically come from Sonneberg in Thuringia, their caves deep in the Ore Mountains. The lush forests provides wood-carving material for the people who live there, the only income for those who make the little trinkets that are like the Dragon who has befriended them. Nutcracker himself is said to have the most powerful of jaws under his thick beard and feeds mostly on nuts given to him as gifts and in exchange provides protection for the townsfolk's that he loves.

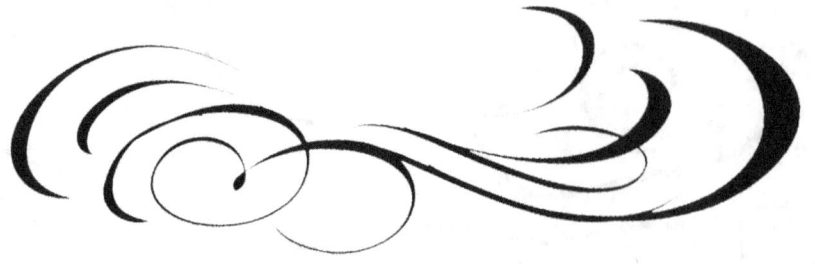

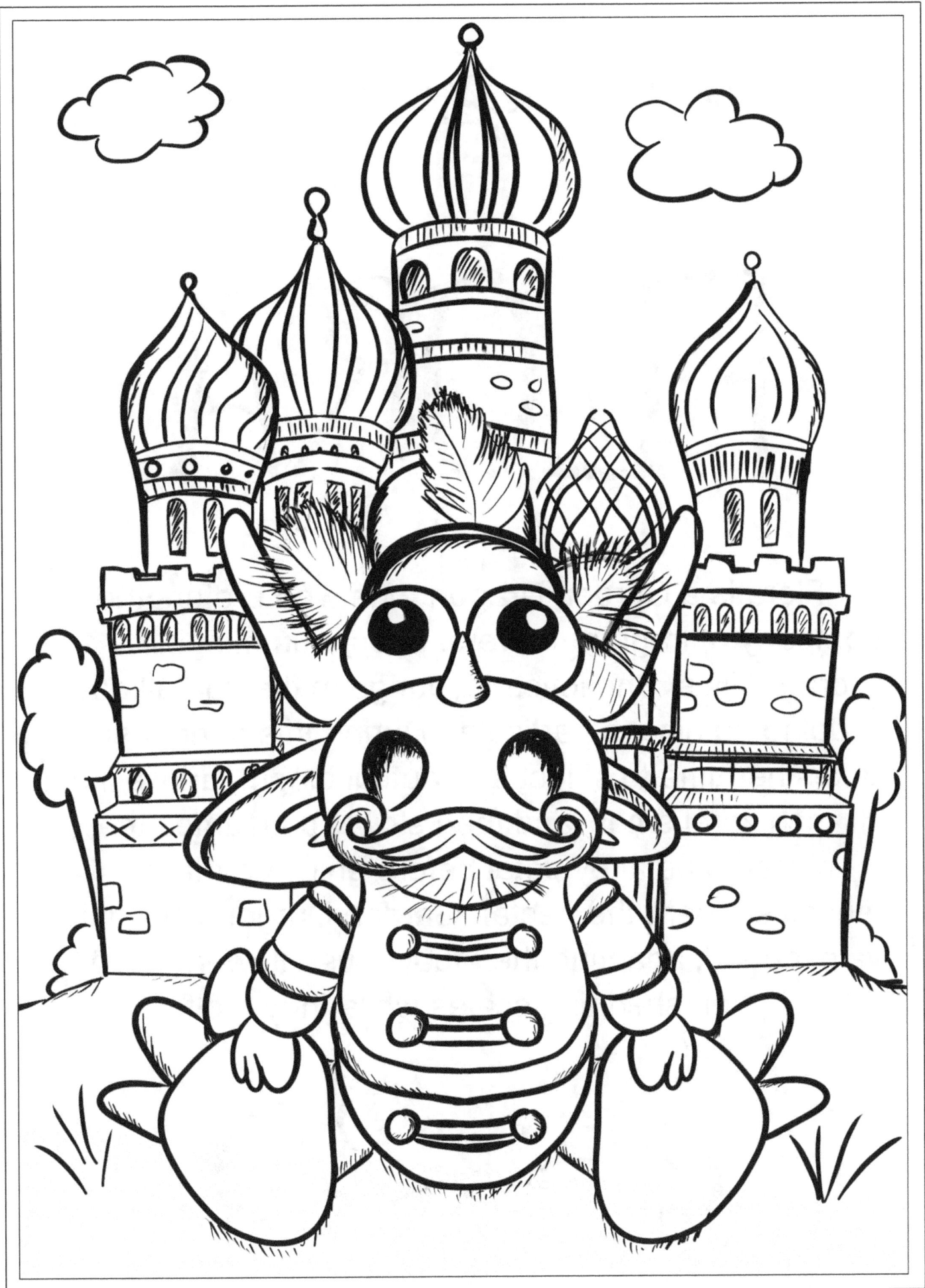

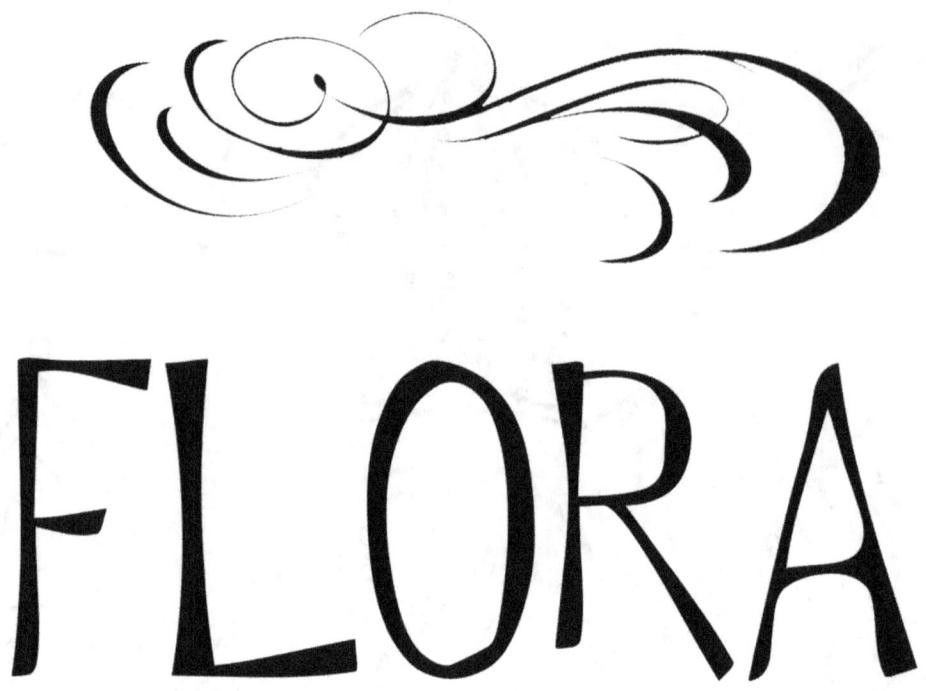

FLORA

Flora is a Garden Dragon, one who prefers the company of fragrant flowers, bees, hummingbirds and dragonflies. She loves to lounge in the sun all day doing nothing in particular. During this period, she takes her time to select a beautiful bloom, drinks in its rich floral smell, and then slowly consumes the blossom petal by petal before enjoying the most succulent part, the nectar. Garden Dragons are quite vain indeed, adapting the ritual to use flowers to cover their shedding scales while they molt.

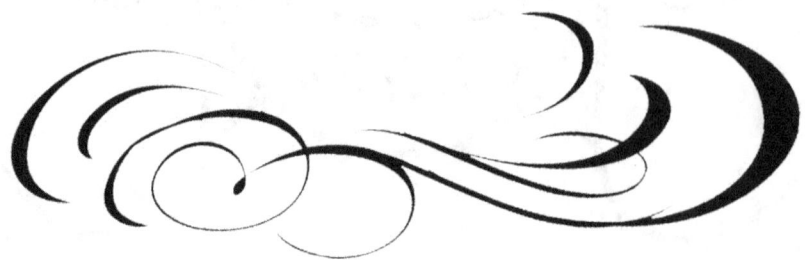

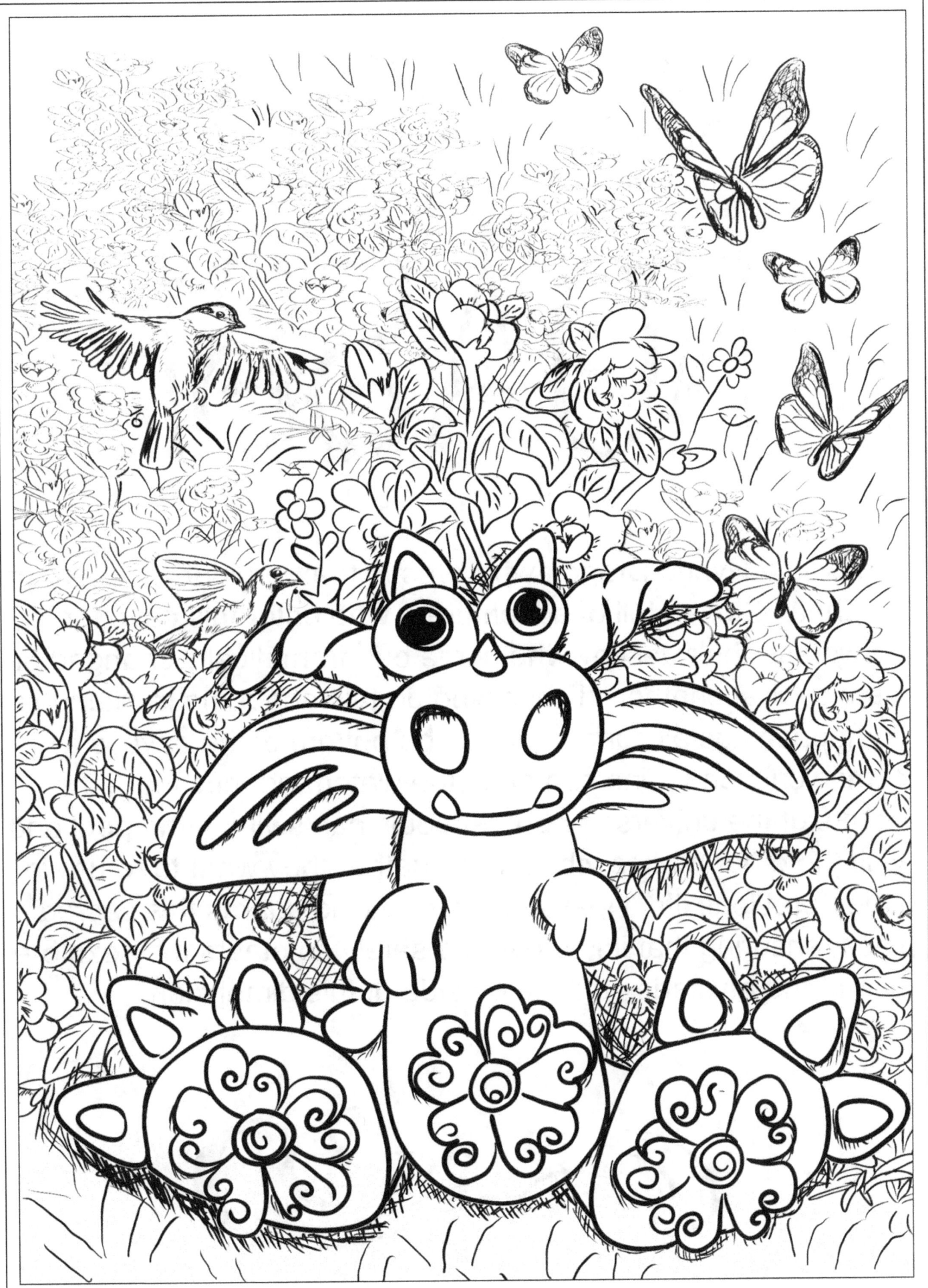

NOASSI

Noassi is a Hybrid Dragon who lives in the Forbidden Cavern of Thaul. Stories tell of adventurers who enter this cave for answers to their destiny who come out dramatically changed or disappear altogether. Those who do talk about the mysterious happenings all concur that at the bottom of the cave is a magical pond. One can drink the water and thus learn the secrets of the universe or braver souls can swim in the pool and visit the other realms, choosing whether they want to return to their previous life. Noassi is the one who guards this sacred place, ensuring that it is protected safely so others may explore the mysteries that lie outside of this dimension.

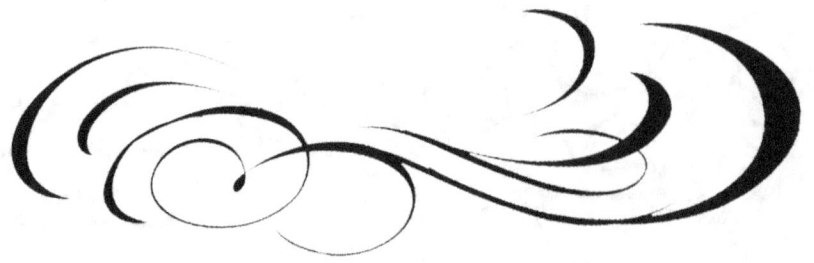

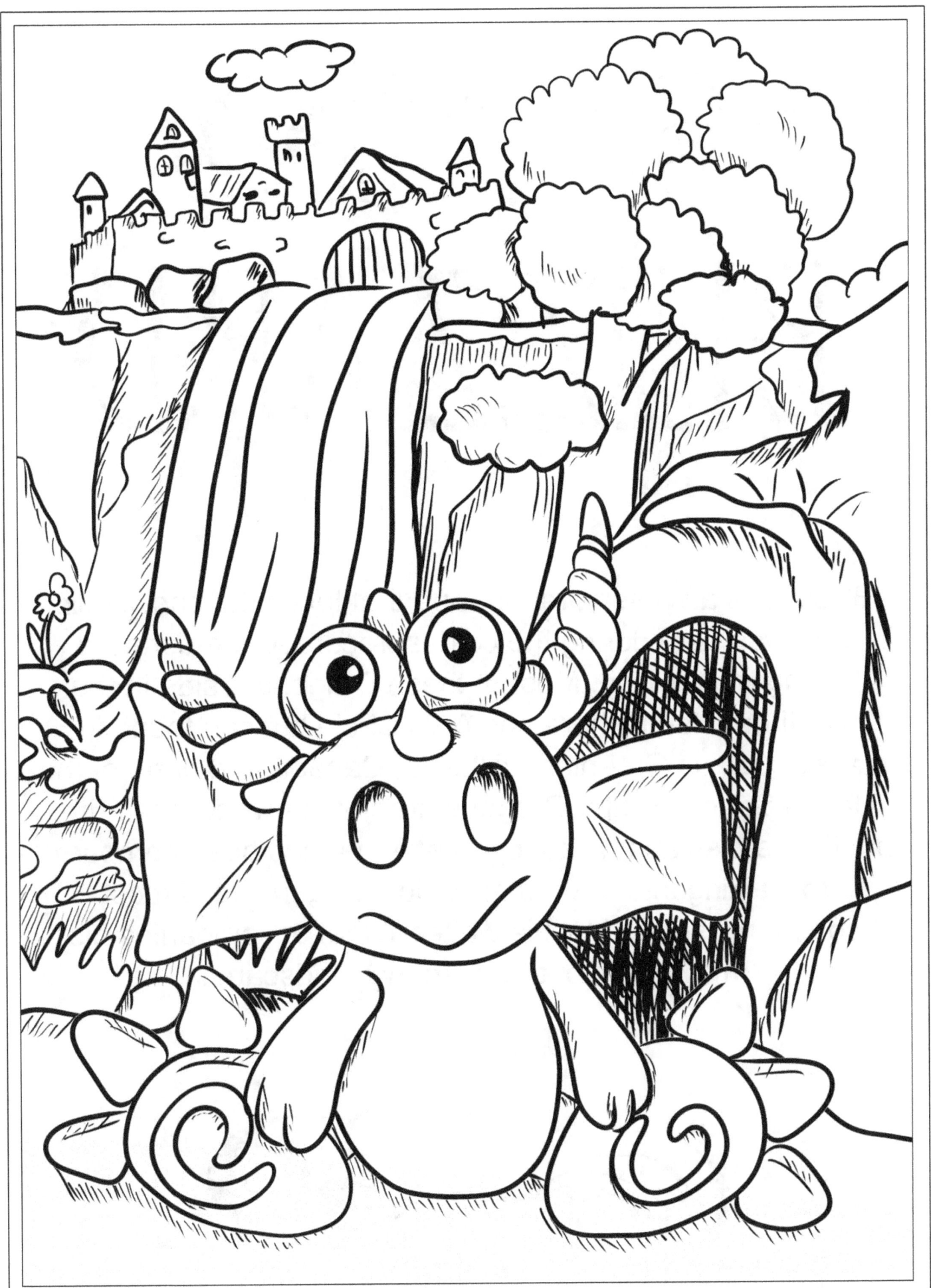

BLIZZARD

Blizzard is a Winter Dragon, one that loves the snow, cold and was born during the coldest recorded temperature during the solstice. Most of these Dragons reside in the Northern Hemisphere and Artic Circle but can found in places such as Greenland, Russia, Canada and parts of the United States. Winter Dragons are not known for their fire, but Blizzard's vapor is an icy freeze that has been compared to walking into a room of liquid nitrogen. He is most commonly spotted by his whiteout that accompanies his movement over the snowy landscape.

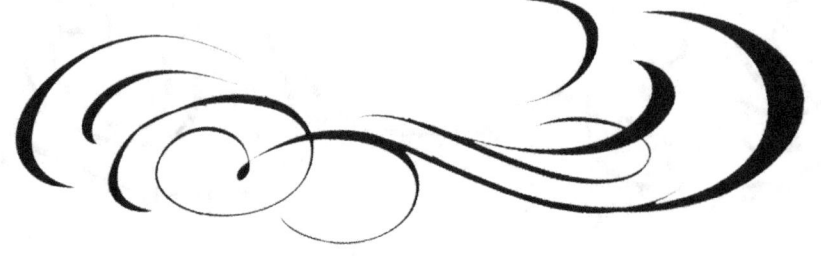

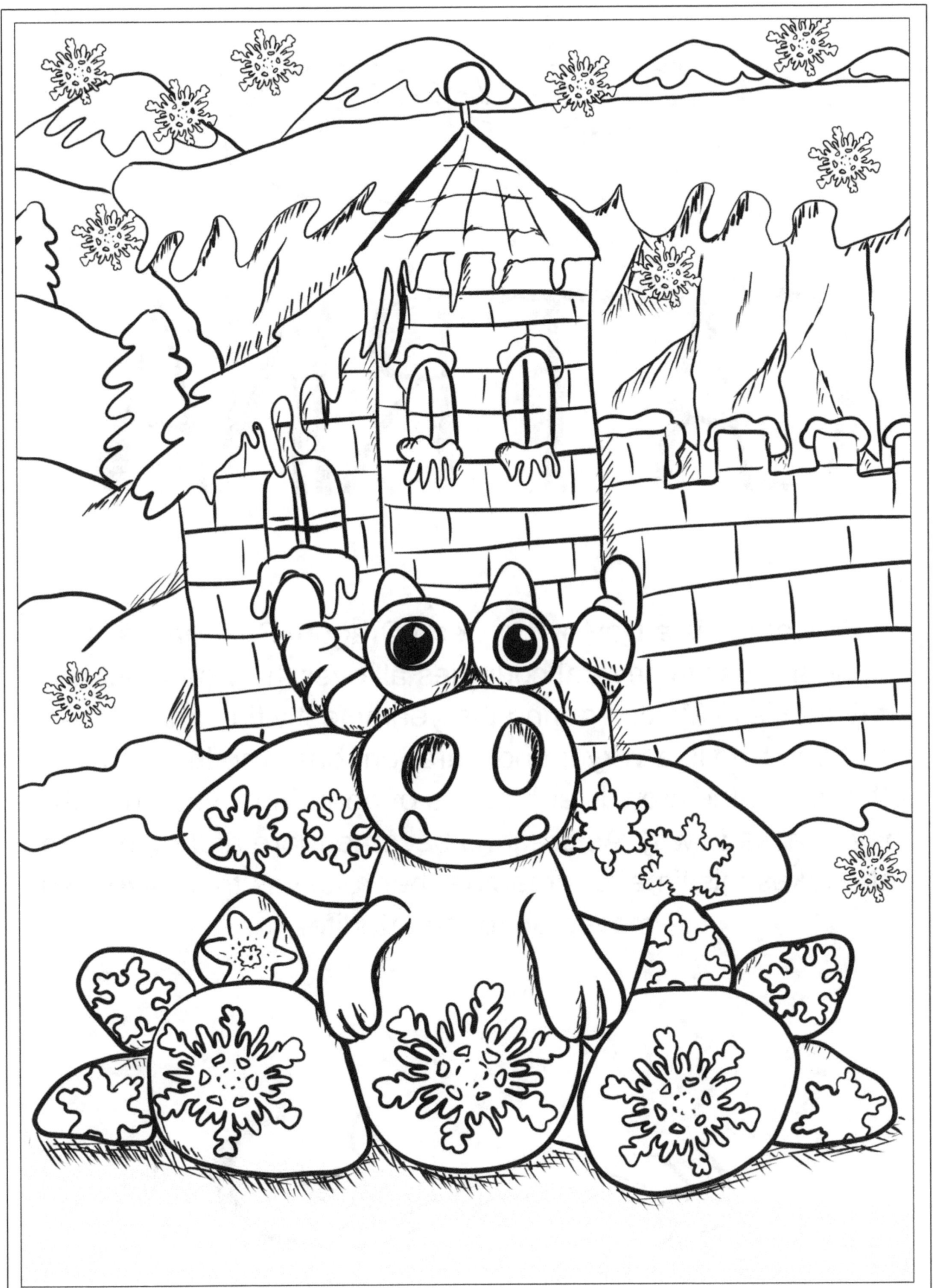

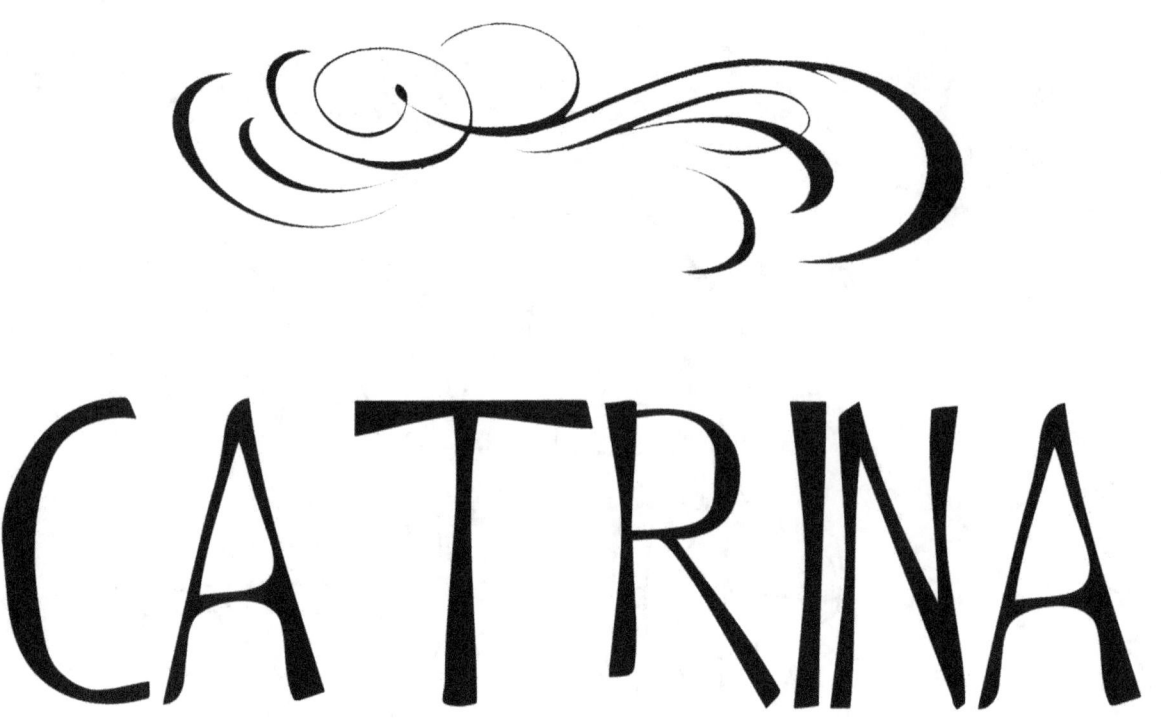

CATRINA

Catrina is a Day of the Dead Dragon. She makes appearances in several countries all over the world, but her favorite is in Mexico during the yearly festivities on October 31st. She is a very friendly dragon, one who loves the attention of the crowds and rituals of honoring loved ones that have passed away. As dragons become more and more rare, she takes this time to remember her relatives that have also moved on to the afterlife.

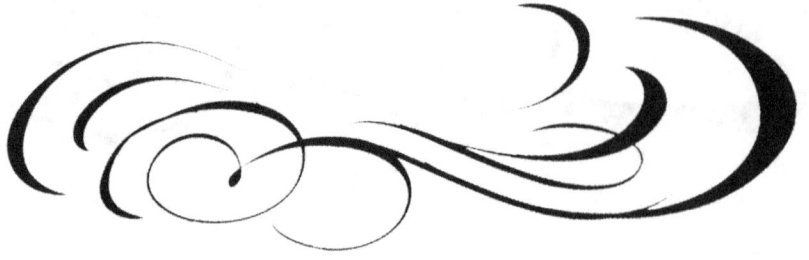

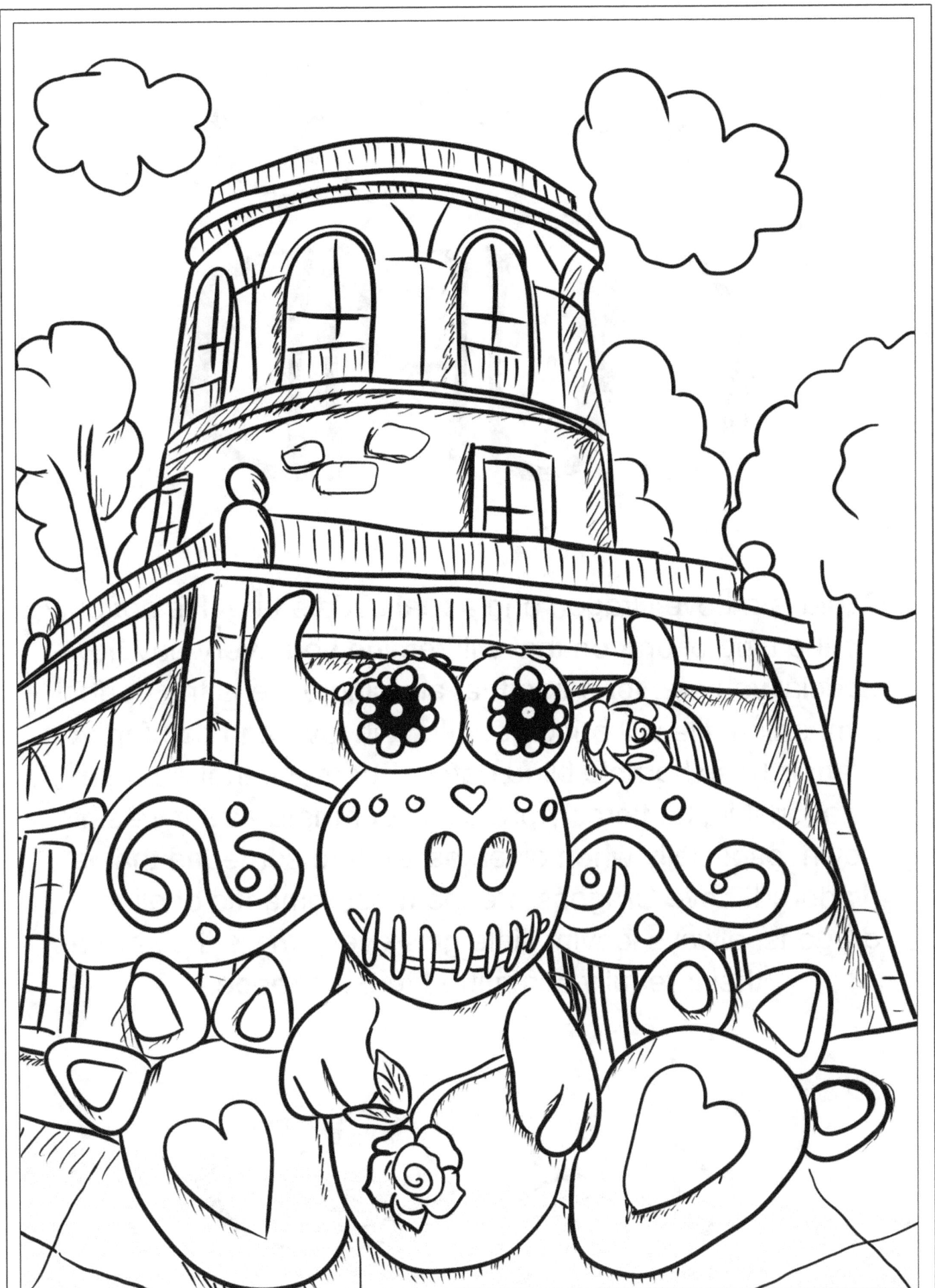

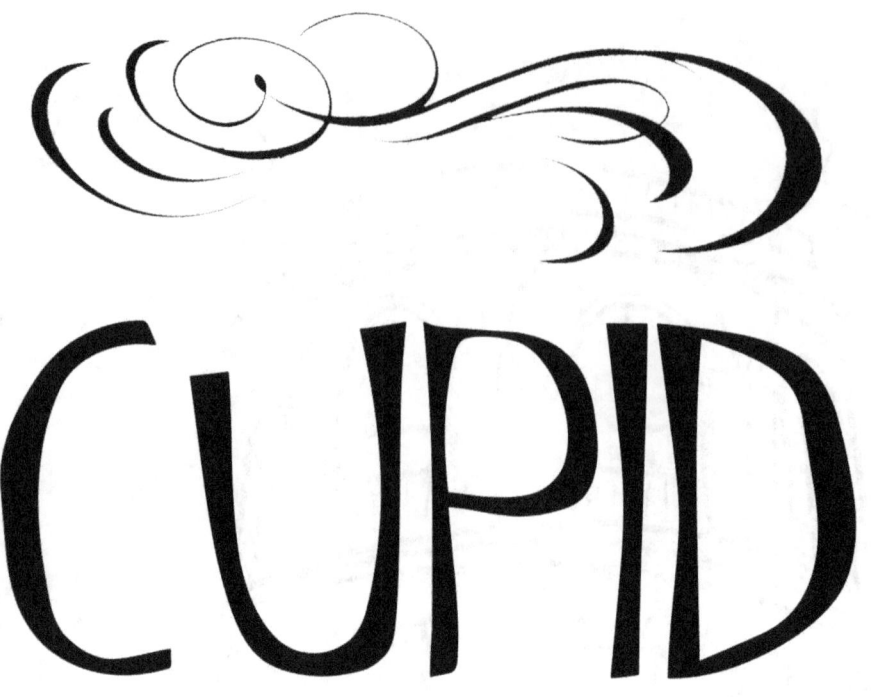

CUPID

Cupid is a Love Dragon and a real cuddle bug! He not only is the type of dragon that will remind you every day how special you are; for those that are single, he is the perfect companion. He will bring good luck in love and comfort you after those horrible blind dates. For those that are in a relationship, he fiercely protects your mate as if it was his own, especially when given as a gift to someone that is adored. Love Dragons are the most romantic of all the dragons, always leaving little gifts everywhere they are as they are fully committed to their keeper.

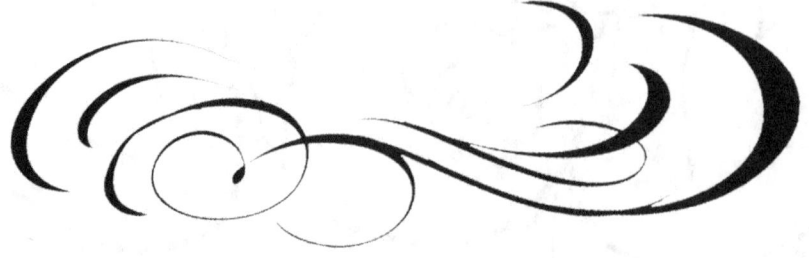

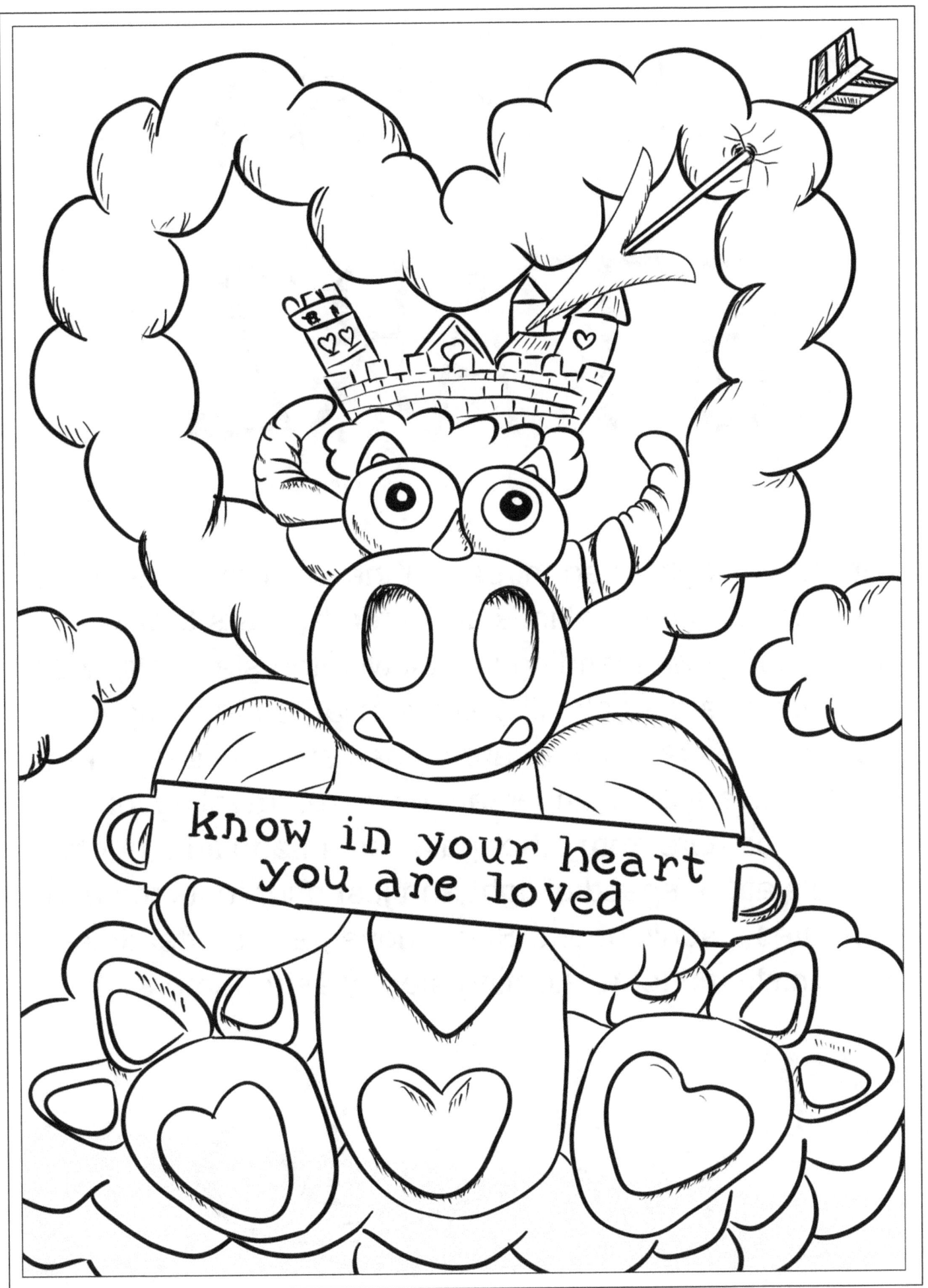

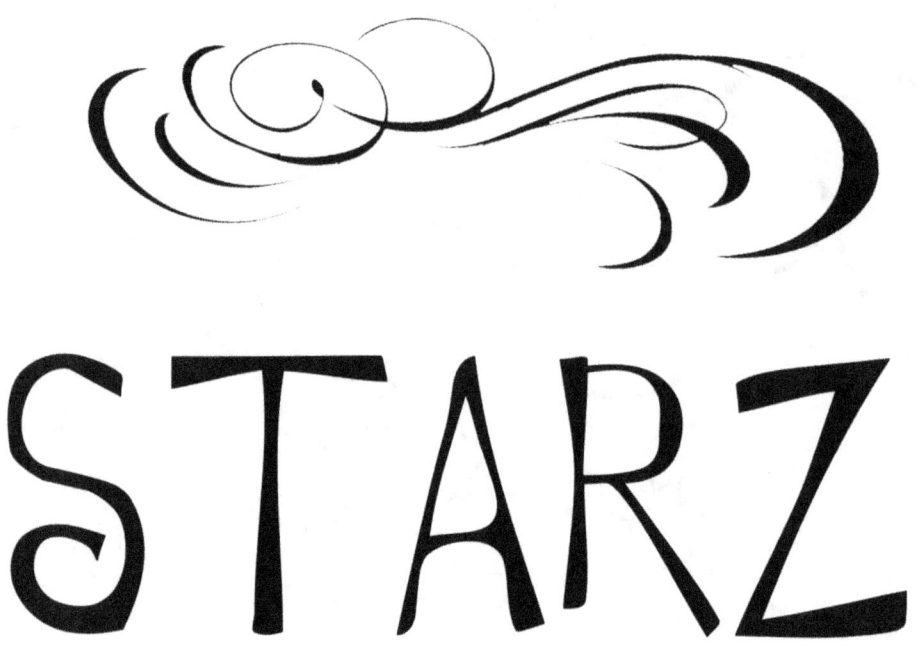

STARZ

Starz is a Night Dragon, part of the universe collection. Her shimmery skin is accented by stars that in darkness glow, blending in well with the starry sky. Her moves are stealth like and similar to other Night Dragons as one of the rarest ones seen. It is rumored they live a thousand years or more, traveling long distances here from other galaxies. In addition, her fire travels at the speed of light and just prior to its release, creates a sonic boom. Starz movement is oftentimes mistaken for a shooting star by astronomers.

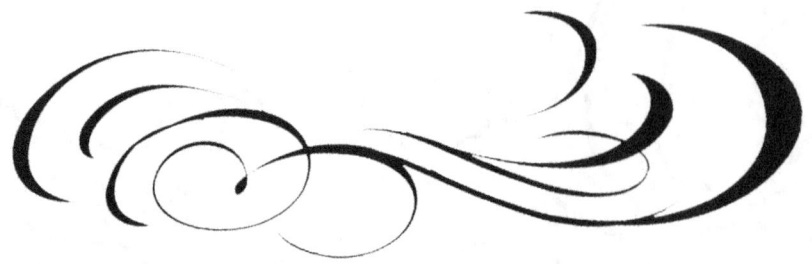

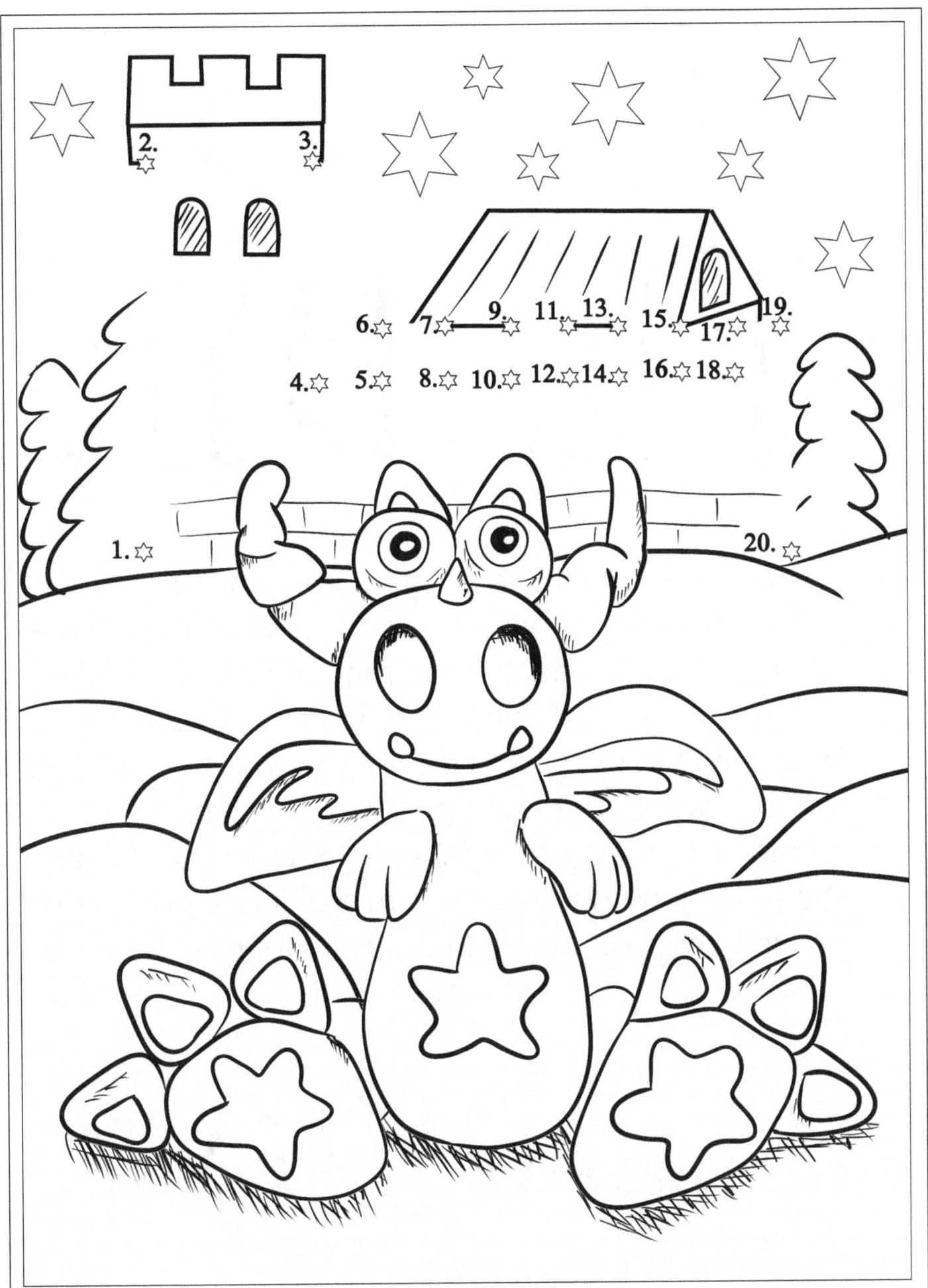

TIE DYE

Tie-Dye is a Hippie Dragon, one whose outer appearance matches her eclectic personality. She is fun loving and laid back, preferring to spend her time in large crowds listening to various musicians and discussing the infinite possibilities of the universe. She is artsy, free-spirited, and peaceful creature. She is for harmony and against violence. Her home is wherever the roads lead her and her circle of friends knows no country or religious boundaries as long as they are serene as herself.

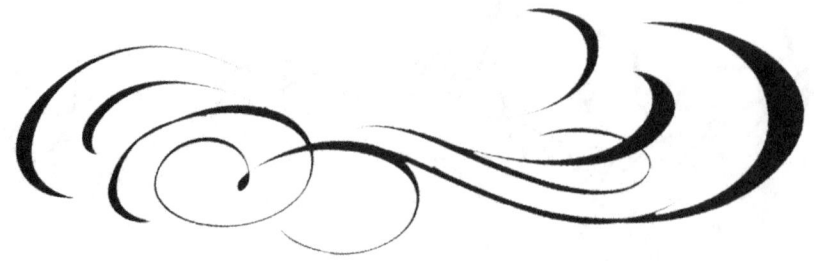

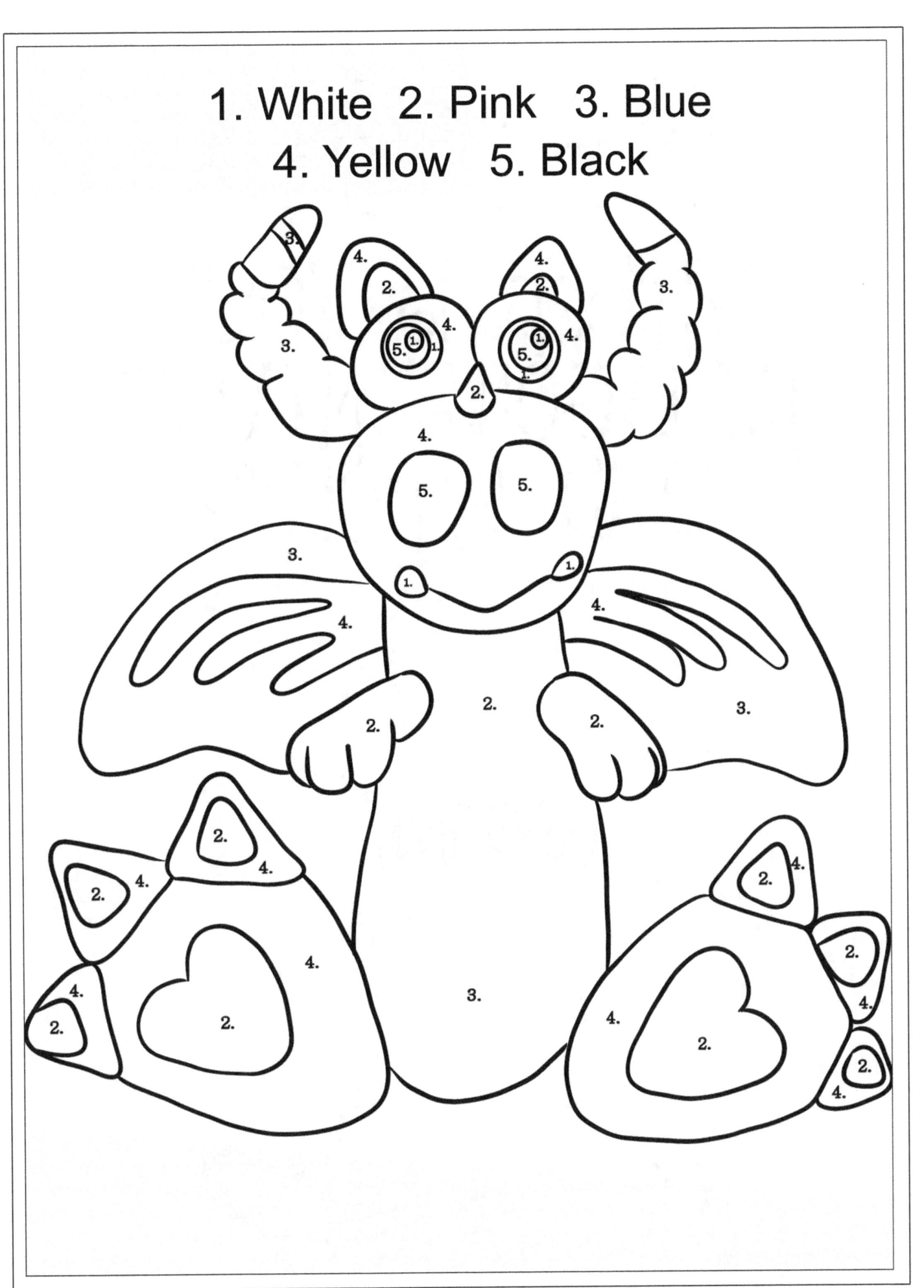

WHAT IS YOUR DRAGON'S NAME AND STORY?

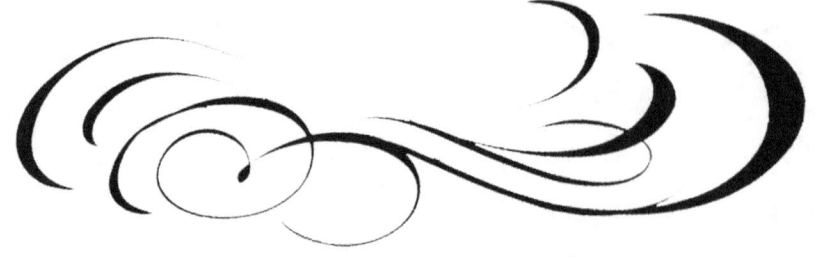

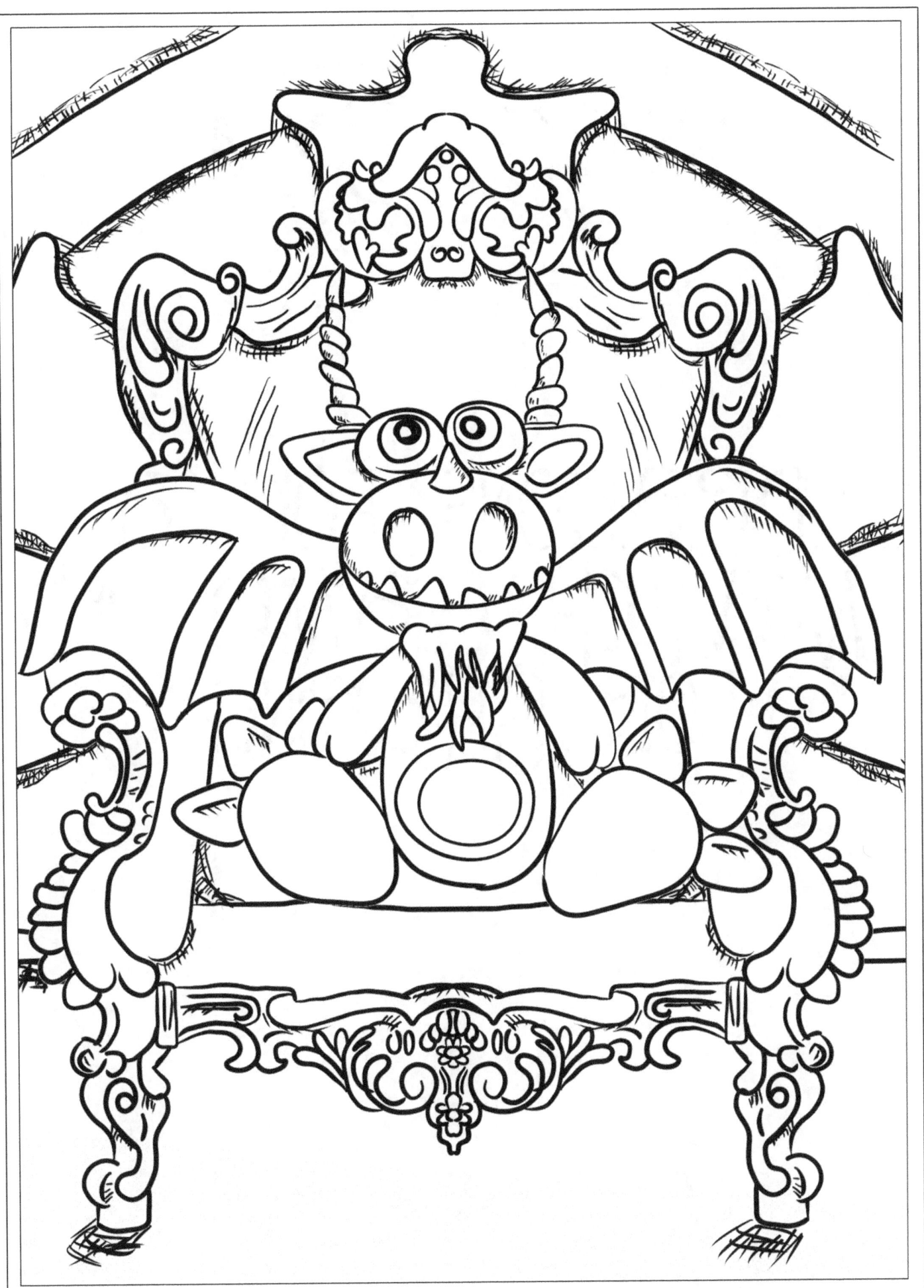

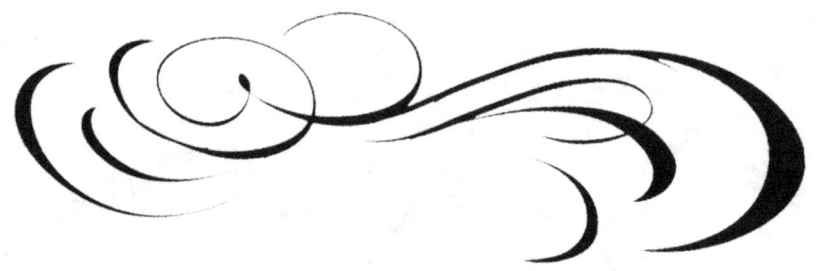

DRAGONS FOR A
MATCH GAME OR
FOR SHARING.

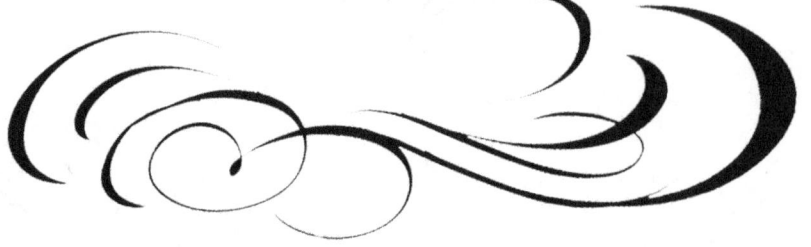

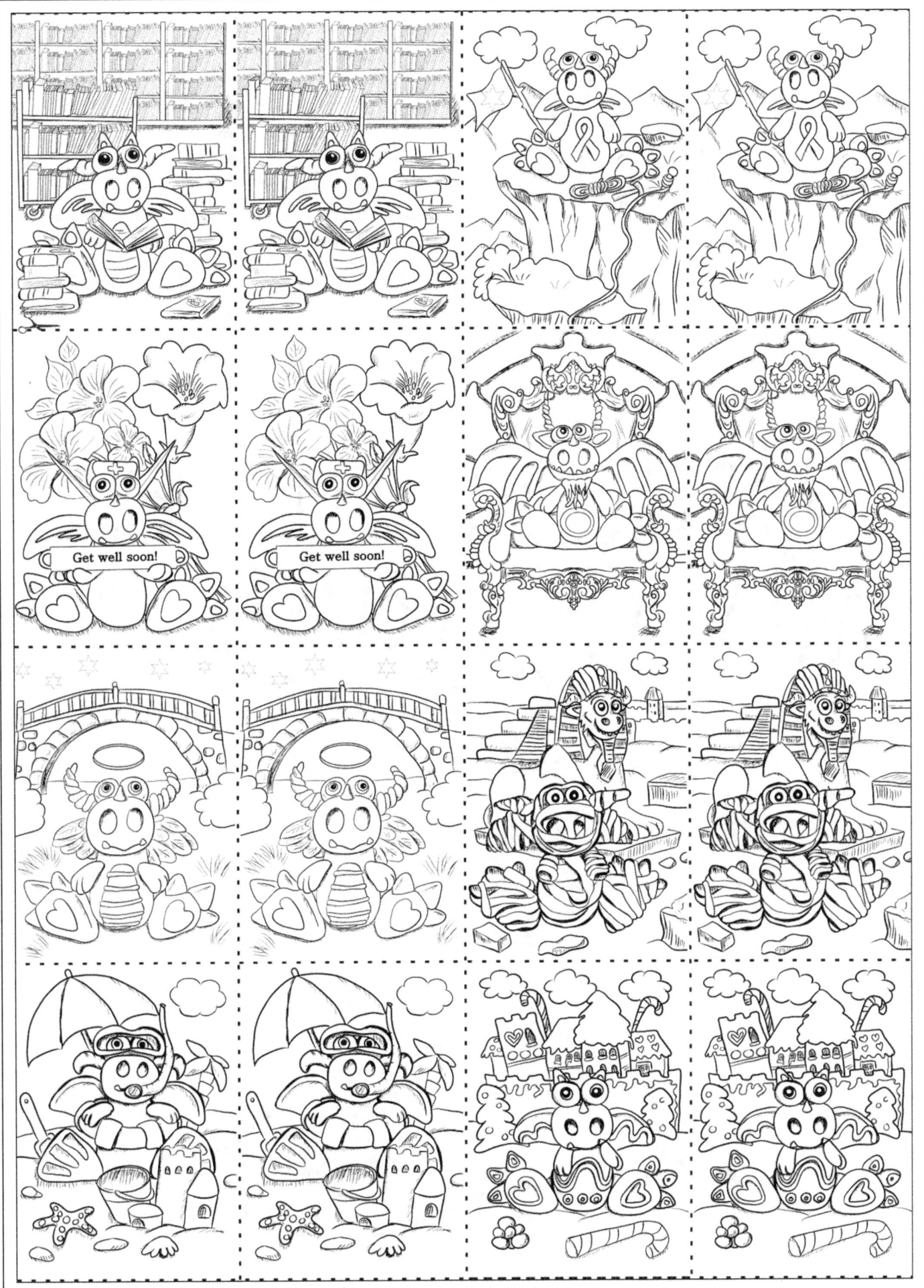

Get well soon!

Get well soon!

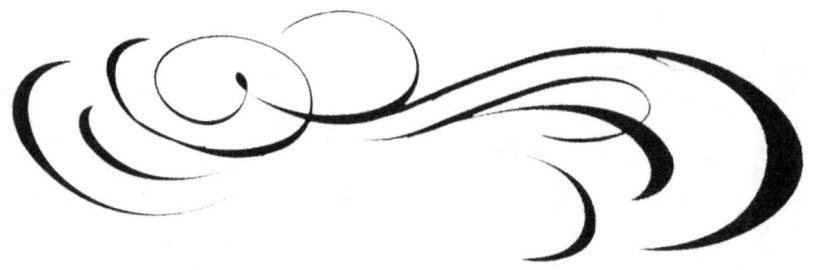

DRAGONS FOR A
MATCH GAME OR
FOR SHARING.

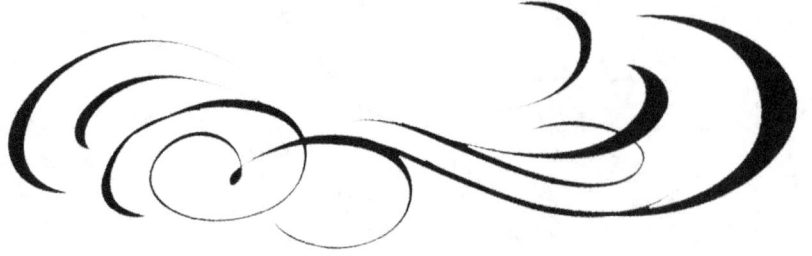

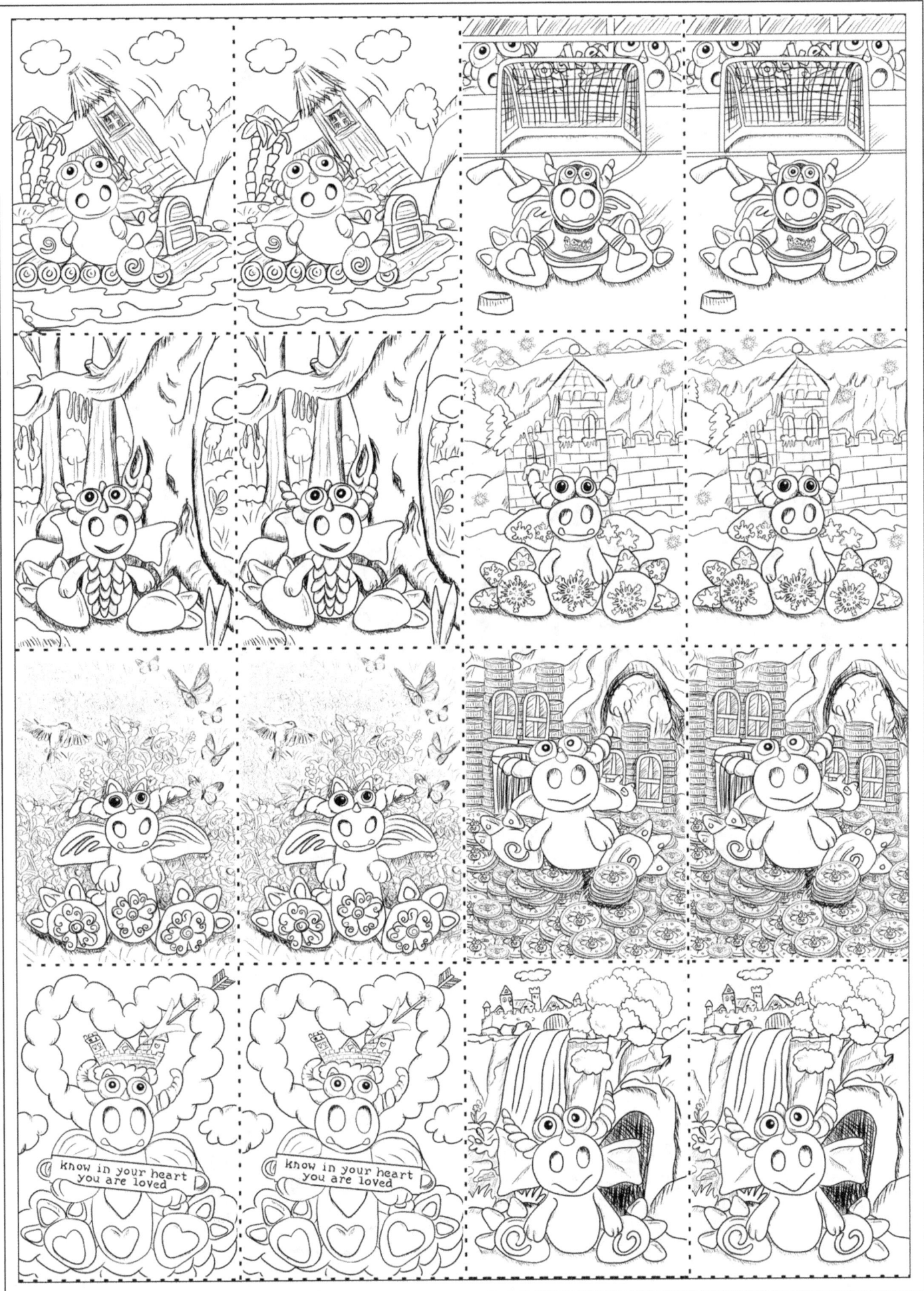

know in your heart
you are loved

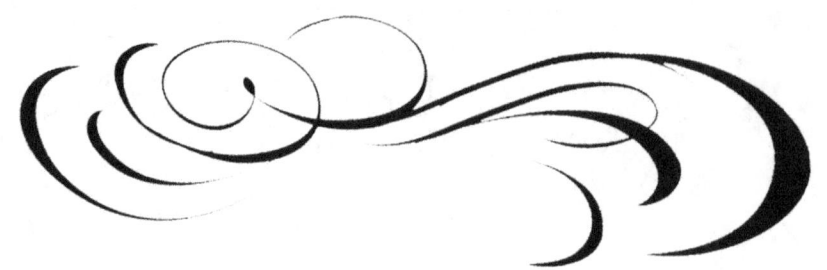

DRAGONS FOR A
MATCH GAME OR
FOR SHARING.

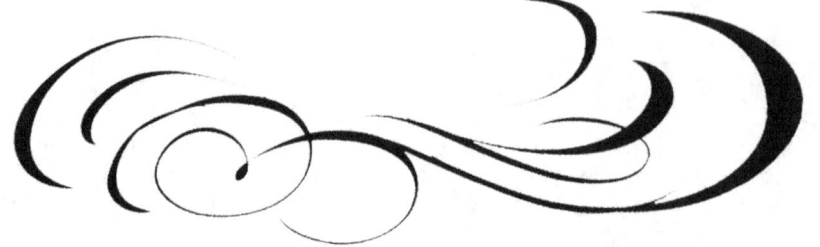

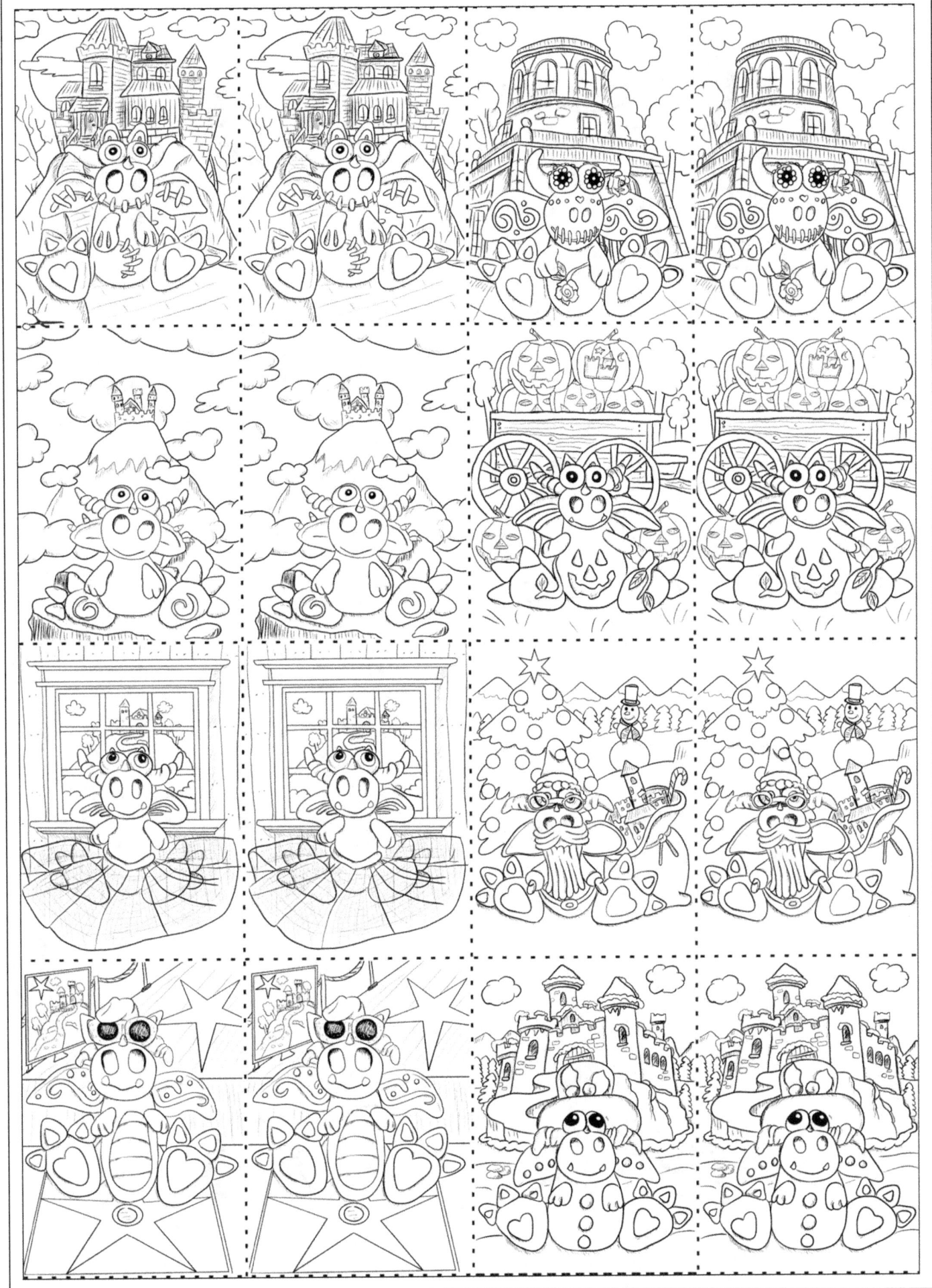

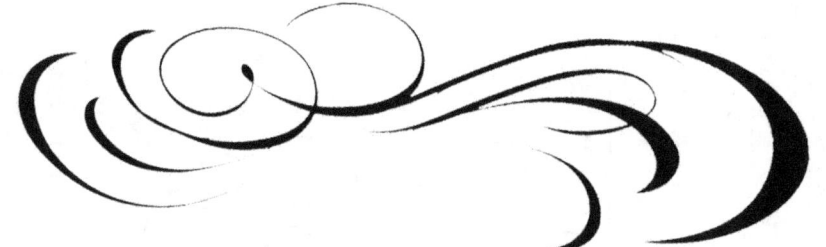

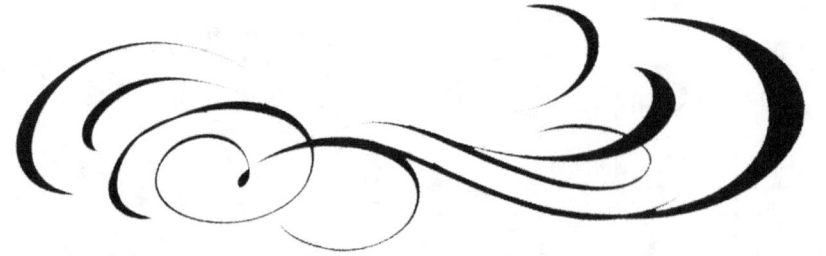